FROM HELL TO THE
—NATIONAL—
HALL OF FAME

ALEXANDRE ELY

STRATTON
—PRESS—
Publishing Life

FROM HELL TO THE NATIONAL HALL OF FAME
Copyright © 2019 **Alexandre Ely**

Stratton Press Publishing
831 N Tatnall Street Suite M #188,
Wilmington, DE 19801
www.stratton-press.com
1-888-323-7009

ISBN (Paperback): 978-1-64345-110-7
ISBN (Ebook): 978-1-64345-393-4

Printed in the United States of America

I'd like to leave a note of thanks to my daughter, Andrea Ely, for typing and helping to correct my manuscript. Thank you to my daughter, Janet Mesquita, for helping me with the editing of this book.

I'd also like to thank good, personal friends of mine from the National Soccer Hall of Fame, Mr. George Brown and his wife, Peggy, for the introduction and advices.

Furthermore, I'd like to express my thanks to my good friends, Wolfgang Finger and his wife, Judy, for their help and advice.

SYNOPSIS

Alex Ely no doubt had an adventurous life, from his birth in Brazil continuing with his voyage to America and ultimately being inducted into the United States Soccer Hall of Fame. Leaving Brazil, he came to America not knowing what his destiny would bring. He strived through the hardships of the average newcomer to America, but he possessed love and talent for the sport of soccer, which took him to places he'd never dreamt about.

Although he faced struggles in many facets of his life, soccer was always the cornerstone that helped him succeed. At seventeen, Alex had to consider his objectives: to go to work as a tradesman or to pursue an education. Not having his parents there to consult with, he decided to go to work and pursue an education at night school. He continued to play soccer despite the obstacles that were in his path. His miraculous elevation to be able to play for the US Pan American, Olympic, and World Cup teams made this young man's dreams come true. Alex was humble and did not realize how important these events were to his life. When selected to be in the Soccer Hall of Fame, he was surprised, but his talent and unique style of playing earned him this well-deserved honor.

FOREWORD

Those of us who know Alex Ely, and considered him a friend, will not be surprised at the refreshing honesty with which he approached this autobiography. His life's journey started in São Paulo, Brazil, where, as the son of German immigrants, his struggle to overcome intolerance and prejudice rested on his soccer skills and his native survival instincts. It continues with his emigration to the US where, as a very young man with no family or friends, he had to find his way in a strange country, dealing with major cultural differences as well as language problems. And he recounts his soccer career, which began with the rough and tumble of Brazilian street soccer up through his Olympic and World Cup accomplishments, culminating in his election to the National Soccer Hall of Fame—the pinnacle of his US soccer.

Along the way, Alex has to overcome many obstacles which were compounded, as he forthrightly acknowledges, by some personal mistakes; but each of them he used as a life lesson from which to move forward. His soccer career is well chronicled in the annals of soccer history but that is simply the skeleton of his life. The back stories in his autobiography, which includes anecdotes about his relationships with soccer legends like Pelé and Kubala, add flesh to his public persona. So, too, do the stories of his successful fight for a college education and his trials and tribulations with organized soccer at the local and national levels.

Alex pulls no punches in recounting his brushes with various individuals in organized soccer and his disagreement with the ruling body's approach to the development and promotion of soccer in the USA. He is equally concerned about the Federation's philosophy of coaching and, more particularly, his perception of the failure to utilize the vast experience of ex-players like himself. Not all will agree with him, but it is vintage Ely—he says what is in his heart.

George Brown
National Soccer Hall of Fame Awardee

INTRODUCTION

As the world turns on its axis, the game of soccer is taking shape all over the world. In Africa, the Middle East, the Orient, South and Central America, and Europe, soccer has developed extensively and is continuing to do so. What has happened in the United States of America? How is it possible for football, baseball, basketball, hockey, golf, tennis, etc., to become bigger than the universal game of soccer? The people running this game elsewhere seem smarter than the people running soccer in the US. They make sure that soccer is not publicized, as it should be. They spread their money around to make sure that soccer doesn't grow. Why? They are already making money and are motivated by such, thus resulting in soccer not getting the popularity that it deserves. This movement started in the 1950s when the USA defeated England in a World Cup game in Brazil. Back then, we had a good chance of making soccer grow, but the US Federation was not able to bring the revolution needed. Soccer is a people sport. The idea of having a single owner never appealed to me.

In South America, the big clubs are associations with a large membership and a board of directors. Here, we have to bow down to some wealthy person who decided to have a professional team for whatever reason it may be. It doesn't make sense to me. However, be that as it may, that is the way it is in America. They do reject soccer because it is the only sport that can cause a disruption of the other sport's dollar earnings as it is all over the world, and it cannot be regulated to their standards. Also, the generation of players from the 1950s to the present seemed to be prefabricated with techniques taught by many foreign groups that came to America, thus limiting the individual plays to their teachings.

I can speak about this subject confidently because I grew up in a country where kids learn by playing and watching good players and they emulate them, thus beating the teaching concept. Talent is not just a word. It belongs to people who dedicate themselves to a game until they pass normal stages and bring new artistic plays into the game. That is the reason Brazil had Pelé and Argentina had Maradona. America is definitely a country that offers the best to candidates for any sport. The youth is ready to learn, but due to many concerns, we don't have the teachers to teach them.

In any country where soccer is a major sport, they use former great players to teach the sport to the youth. This doesn't work in America because the game is considered foreign and has been passed to British or Australian coaches who failed over there and are trying to make some money here. We are also creating an era of coaches who did not live the game but like it, so they get the job.

In my coaching days, I always produced winners and never got recognized for it. There are always candidates who are able to create a fantastic résumé on paper with pictures and all the ingredients that they need to give them credentials for a job that they know nothing about. Of course, the athletic directors are not really concerned about soccer, so they don't really care who they bring in as soccer coaches around whose doors were shut for them.

I wasn't shy to learn from Mr. Lajos Varga, a Hungarian coach of the Ukrainian Nationals in the early 1960s. As I propelled through my soccer life, I felt not wanted by many in the soccer world. I felt the lack of respect everywhere. It is like frying an egg on your forehead. Our USSF (United States Soccer Federation) is the first to place you where you can't hurt them. They are followed by the individual owners of the professional clubs then by most athletic directors of universities and colleges. We have a group of coaches schooled by the US Soccer Association who are teaching coaches in America the same way that they had learned. They share most of the Federation jobs. What else is there that can be said without hurting the actual crew's feelings? I am sure they are doing their best, but it may not be enough. Under these conditions, it will take another twenty years for soccer to grow, perhaps due to the population change or some other miracle. I can't foresee any big change in the next five years. For all the people who love soccer, let's hope that there will be changes and the game will grow regardless of the negativity around it. Soccer is a superior sport that can change countries and people.

CHAPTER ONE

I was born Alexandre Ely in the town of Mogy das Cruzes in the state of São Paulo, Brazil. My father, Edward Ely, owned a farm in that area and was attempting to make a living by transporting produce grown in the farm to the city of São Paulo. He was a German immigrant who participated in World War I. He also had endured the hardships of warfare at a very young age and was wounded fighting in the trenches against the Russians. The doctors gave him three months to live, but Edward bounced back. Then he decided to move far away from the turmoil in Europe; he chose Brazil for its being a new and promising land.

In 1938, Brazil was a young and wild country colonized by the Portuguese. Brazil became independent from Portugal in the 1820s. Many Portuguese loved Brazil and refused to return to Portugal. Consequently, they left their language and their culture in Brazil. Brazil inherited many other things from Portugal, including soccer, a sport that was to become famous in Brazil.

Even before I was five years old, my father decided to sell the farm and move to São Paulo, Brazil. During that time, a new war broke out in Europe, and Germany was involved. My father did not want to get involved, but because we were of German ancestry, we were targeted by people around us. I was six years old when four Brazilian men who wanted to kill my entire family invaded my house. My father came out to the yard with a wooden cable and beat these men until three of them died right there on the spot. One of them somehow escaped. After that horrible incident, we then received protection from the authorities until the end of the war.

Brazil was rich in many things, but the people there lived poorly. Right after the World War II, my family started a general store, a business that was needed there at that time. The local people came from all around to buy necessary items. They stood in lines in front of the store. Most items were sold on credit. The buyers had their names placed in account books to be paid at the end of each month. Needless to say, my father never saw any of that money. There were hundreds of names in those accounts. They thought that because of my father's German ancestry, it was all right not to pay him. We were unwanted foreigners in Brazil at that time. There were some other Europeans around who didn't care for Germans either. They also became our enemies.

Two houses down the block, there were some Lithuanian people who displayed greater hate toward us than the other people. They insulted us and became violent by threatening our family. One afternoon, my mother, Elsie, was going downtown; as she waited for the bus, for no apparent reason, this insane Lithuanian lady attacked her. I was just a little boy witnessing all this violence. My mother struggled with that lady as they rolled on the ground until she got a handful of her hair and ripped it right off her skull. This made the lady stop and run home. I was just a kid, victimized by hatred from people I didn't even know.

Since my family became established there, I made some local friends as time flew by. Since the streets at that time were unpaved, I spent some time roaming around, playing with other kids, and learning Portuguese. At home though, we spoke mostly German and broken Portuguese. Young kids had little to do other than play in the streets. Our street was coming from a main street called Estrada do Vergueiro, which ended up on a highway that led to Santos after descending a *serra* (mountain) for almost one hour. Santos is Pelé's land, where he started his career in the Santos FC.

As kids, we learned soccer by playing street games and watching neighborhood teams and professional teams whenever possible. On my street lived mixed players of all colors and races. There was even one kid called *rato branco* (white rat) due to his beyond-white color. These kids can hardly see the soccer ball on the sunny days. At that time, there was no organized soccer being played there.

My father always stood by the store door, watching the kids play. Every now and then, there was a fight; and when I was involved, my father never helped me. He wanted me to learn how to fight my own battles.

At that time, our street was called Rua (street), which later, after being paved, changed to São Daniel Street, which is its name today. It is in the same neighborhood called Vila Brasilio Machado, which now changed to Saude District.

One day, I was playing soccer in the street when a fight broke out. It was me against a black kid named Lanerde. I got beat up pretty badly, so I went to my father's store crying and looking for help. My father said, "You get back there and give him what he gave you." I was scared, but I went back in the street and fought again until I finally defeated the kid. Lanerde thought I was crazy and called me a "crazy" German. I started to feel more grown-up and strong, finding ways to defeat my enemies. This is a characteristic that I acquired in the streets, which later helped me with soccer. Sometimes the kids played soccer all day long, taking no breaks to eat or drink. For most of the time, we were barefoot, with no shirts and just a pair of shorts. We learned how to fake, shoot, and do just about anything with the homemade balls of socks or anything that was close enough and round enough to be kicked.

Most of the kids learned soccer by playing it constantly. I developed a liking for the game all on my own. My father hated the game and did everything possible to keep me away from it, but he was unable to do it. I used to play with a tennis ball in my yard, imagining that I was in a stadium full of people. That was just a dream. Sometimes we would find a real field and play the entire field two on two. We would run back and forth all day long until it got dark.

In Brazil, many times I felt like a foreigner even though I was born there. Growing together with the neighborhood kids, I began to learn some of their behaviors, including some that weren't good.

There were gangs that were attacking and robbing people, and many of those guys were my friends from soccer.

My parents tried to put me in a highly rated school as an intern in Colegio São Bento in center city São Paulo. I stayed there for two years. German priests headed the school. I became a rebellious kid, getting in trouble constantly for fighting. The teachers were constantly punishing me by making me stay in a room and copy the articles from a *regulation* book that they had. One Wednesday, my mother came to visit me while they kept me in a room doing my punishment. I ran away dying to see my mother while there was a cowboy movie on. The *vigilantes* (disciplinarians) came down looking for me. They stopped the movie, turned the lights on, and found me hugging my mother with the theater almost full of people. I was longing for my mother and the other members of my family. It was a strong longing, one that turns you into a vegetable.

One night, out of fear, some kid snuck unto the bed of another kid. Immediately, I was accused and called irresponsible, etc. I was then called into the office and mistreated because that type of accusation was very serious. Later they found out it wasn't me, but I still felt the pain and severity of that situation. The only real pleasure that I had in this school in São Paulo was during gym class when we played soccer. I wasn't a good swimmer, so on one occasion, I nearly drowned. Another young kid who also loved soccer saved me. By the amount of money that my parents paid for my education, I wasn't getting it in any way. I did not like that school's environment; so my mother first took me out from being an intern and made me an extern, that is, I had to travel every day to that horrible school.

Finally, due to the distance and other problems, I was moved to a local high school called São Francisco Xavier. Japanese teachers basically ran it. I soon started cutting classes, and my parents were upset when they found out, so at the age of fifteen, I was taken out of student life and put to work in downtown São Paulo as a messenger boy for a photographer, Mr. DeBoer, a Dutchman who worked with the largest companies in São Paulo. He was a technical photographer, one of the best. The responsibility of the job encouraged me to enter night school. That was a big change in my life because I began to feel more responsible and was able to play soccer on the weekends.

In my neighborhood, we played four games every Saturday and Sunday. At sixteen, I was playing with the men's teams, and it was a tough deal because to be accepted by the fans and players was very difficult. There were people who actually believed in my talent. They tried to convince me to try out for a professional team. I did it once and was very disappointed. The coach at that time was a black man named Charuto, which means cigar. There were many kids at the tryout, and most of them were black, and the coach seemed happy with their performances. He never said a word to me, so I never went back. In Brazil, many of the kids looked forward to playing pro soccer because they were not prepared for anything else, and that was the only way to gain notoriety and money doing what they enjoyed the most.

CHAPTER TWO

Learning soccer is just like learning any other activity except that to become a professional player, you need a lot more preparation and skill. I started playing on the streets with my bare feet. My opponents were street kids just like me. We would play every day on our free time. Sometimes we played at night, which was rather challenging back in those days. When you play soccer like we did, you learn naturally how to maneuver the ball with different spins and good quality ball control.

I had never worn a soccer shoe until I was twelve, and it was tough to find one that fit me. It took me months to adjust to playing soccer with shoes on. The soccer shoe plays an important role in a soccer player. One needs to adjust to it. If your shoe is too tight, it makes your moves difficult and your running is changed considerably, thus making your game pay for it. At the time that I was growing, shoes were expensive and hard to get. When I found shoes that fit me, I wore them until holes appeared in them. I felt that they helped me play well. I had never played a real game until I was thirteen years old. As I mingled with the street kids playing soccer, I learned of the many illegal activities that some of them were doing. They robbed people and placed their lives in danger constantly. Every so often, one of them would get shot. Some recovered, but others died really stupidly or got crippled for life. They were poor with no jobs available to them and no chance to advance through school or work. Lots of them merely went by their lives, not knowing where or when their time would come. By hanging around and keeping my mouth shut, I sort of became trusted by them.

One of the things that helped me was joining the samba school we created around the neighborhood. I had learned the *batucada* (Brazilian samba beat), a Brazilian carnival dance, and I played the *frigideira* (a frying pan used to follow up the samba beat) frying pan or I danced in front of it as an abre alas, which means "open the way for the school to pass by." We paraded around the neighborhood first, and when we got better, we went to town where thousands of people watched us and applauded our samba playing. There I was, as one of the *abre alas* (samba school term for people in charge of opening the way), going in front and dancing to the music being played. Anyone who did not move from the front of our way was brought down with a *rasteira* (kick to bring you down to the floor), which means a "kick under you to throw you off balance." I got really good at this and believe that it helped me greatly with soccer. When the people in front of us didn't move then, often fights occurred. Thank God there were no guns involved.

Some of these fights were like gang fights where you could get seriously hurt. One of them occurred in Avenida São Joao downtown. There were two different groups marching in different directions, taking up the entire width of the street, a moment in which our *abre alas* people came face-to-face with the other samba school. There was a display of *pernada* (using legs to bring people down), using your legs against one another. I confronted a kid who was pretty good. He got a few kicks on my head, but I was quick and got him back. Some of our leaders were strong black men who loved to play these samba instruments and were on the right rhythm all the time. They developed a respect for me because I was almost like them. The difference was that I was German-looking, but even so, I still behaved like them. I remember the drummer Moises, who, in later years, was killed in a bar fight. He was also a good soccer player. In fact, many of those young men were decent soccer players. The following year, we were running out of instruments so we started using instruments from another group nearby. Our plan was to get them playing with us, and when they got to trust us, we would get into a fight with them and steal their newer instruments. There were rows of large drums and *pandeiros*, small drums made of animal skins that were worth quite a bit of money. It was on a Saturday when we joined with the other group, and we were all prepared to steal their instruments. We marched up Vergueiro Street to a bus stop called "twenty-two." When we got there, the fight started and all of their instruments were stolen, and their guys got a severe beating on top of it. That is how the beginning of a much larger samba school started. The name chosen was *Academicos do Ipiranga*, which later paraded during many a carnival. This was the very beginning of that samba school.

This subject differs from soccer, but it is connected in many ways because the legs and dexterity come from practice, and there is nothing more enjoyable than to mix rhythm with soccer. The game has to have rhythm, and your body and legs must learn how to follow it.

When Pelé started his career, he had the rhythm and audacity to do many things that players don't dare to do. I was a daring player, except in the USA, a country that did not recognize the game as in Brazil. In fact, during my playing years, I got more publicity in Brazil than in the USA.

Our neighborhood was one of the toughest places to grow up in due to the growing numbers of people being raised with no education and the very deep competition for survival. Since I was part of the group, they never robbed our house or bar. I felt that was because of my being together with them most of my free time. There were some defiant guys around, and every now and then, they would challenge you to a fight. So if you chickened out, you were out of the group. One day when we were playing a street soccer game, a young black man simply came and took the ball away and said the game was over. So most of the guys playing were upset, including myself. I asked him in the best way I could to give us the ball back, but this guy was determined not to let us continue. He was in his higher teens and quite strong, but I got tired of his attitude; and being a lot younger and smaller, I decided to fight the guy anyway. I found out that his name was Reinaldo, and I gave him enough time to return the ball; but he refused to do it. So I jumped at him and started punching and kicking, but he was big and strong. He hit me a few times, but I didn't give up. I kept on fighting until he got tired of hitting me and gave us the ball back so we could continue our game. Since then, Reinaldo, who was one of the leaders of the local gang, began to respect me. He said he admired my courage and lack of fear. He picked on many other guys and kicked their asses, but he left me alone. In fact, later when we grew up, I came to visit his house and ate rice and beans made by his mother on a primitive fire of bricks and coal put together in a square manner to keep the fire under the pan. These experiences helped me to gain some manhood at an early stage in my life.

One summer day, a dangerous group of *favela* (slums), people who live in cardboard houses and don't pay taxes, came to our neighborhood and were looking for one of our guys named Oliveira. They found him and beat him up real good. The people found out and tried to discover who dared invade our neighborhood, knowing that there were consequences for that action. That event put us in a state of war. Our gang now wanted revenge. They were planning to get all the guys together and invade the *vergueiro favela* and let them know who we were so that they would never try that stunt again. They decided to do it on a Saturday because there were more people available. They joined as a war group with weapons. Some of them had guns and *ronqueiras* (homemade guns). They had chains, sticks of wood, tool cables, and whatever else they could find to use as weapons. They were ready at ten in the morning on Saturday to catch them while they were still asleep. So we marched toward the *favela* with close to one hundred guys. When we got there, it was around eleven in the morning. We invaded their *favela*, and everyone who came around took a severe beating, including women and children. Some of our guys were merciless. They delivered their message so well that we never heard from the *favelados* again. All of that gave the people of Vila Brasilio Machado a name, and not many people dared to go there to try any type of revenge. By that time, the police were aware of what was going on, but they didn't arrest anyone. They were already making more rounds around the neighborhood. Some of the guys were arrested later but soon after set free. So they were allowed to continue living their lives as their situation provided.

CHAPTER THREE

I never learned how to appreciate most of the coaches whom I've had. It may be because of my background and my unique way of playing. From most of the coaches, I never learned anything. However, I can remember three men who were fair men and from whose teachings I learned something. I am referring to a young black coach who coached me from the ages of thirteen to fifteen years old. His name was Neno; he was young, nice-mannered, and very much of a man compared to others.

In Brazil, many deviant fellows loved to coach young kids so they can enjoy watching kids undress for games and take showers, thereby invading soccer with lewd purposes. I've seen many fellows around who were like that in Brazil and in the US even in our days. It is hard to accept some of these men, but they were out there, involved with coaching young kids. That made us appreciate good coaches like Neno even more.

My coach Neno decided to get a group of young players and make a soccer team. But it was not just anyone that he was selecting; he was careful that the players he chose were good and had a chance in the pro leagues. We got one training session a week and played our games on Sundays. He selected teams that played in small stadiums and good soccer fields. This team was called União SC, and in a short time, they built a name for themselves. Many more organized teams beat us, but we gave them good games.

Neno wasn't very tolerant with some of the players. If he felt that the player had done a wrong thing, his manner of showing how displeased he was, was to put both open hands on the player's face and lightly slap him. I saw him doing it to a lot of the guys; he would come around smiling and then lightly slapped the guy's face. It was humiliating because the other guys thought it was funny. Then he told the player what he thought and hoped that would not happen again. Thank God I was never punished like that. He respected me as a player. He had me playing middle field on the left side. I was a strong player and derived that from the practices at the samba school. Sometimes we played against older teams, and we gave them a run for their money.

Neno worked for the post office in downtown São Paulo. There he had many connections that helped him in organizing his team and game schedule. There is an area in São Paulo called Horto Florestal (forest plantation), where the city had a lot of grounds some with vegetation and others with room for soccer fields. We played against their junior team. They were very well prepared physically and mentally. We wore white uniforms and looked great, but they still defeated us 3 to 1. It was one of the better games I played, persistently defending and attacking. Most of our players had nicknames; some of the ones that I recall are Fumaca, Ico, Nelson, Ze de Venda, Celso, and Ezio. This team brought together the street players from different neighborhoods, which later made us friends.

Neno also coached the men's team called União E.C., in which he had mostly black players. They also got to play better games due to Neno's connections. My father had a big truck, and he was hired to drive them to different fields. We played a game in the wealthy part of town. They had a beautiful field, and next to it was a movie house. It started to rain while they were playing, and a fight broke out in the field. Since it was the other team's field, we ran in all directions. I somehow got into the movie house, and I was forced to watch a movie with Gary Cooper until the players calmed down.

One afternoon, we played a game against a famous amateur team called Vila Primavera E.C. of São Paulo Guaianazes. They had an excellent team. Only one player was very different in the other team. He was a very fat center-forward. I was a kid watching the game, and I wondered what he was doing out there. After all, we had lots of fit guys. Our goalie was tall, skinny, black fellow named Canela. As the game progressed, their team was always serving the fat guy. Mostly he controlled the ball and delivered good passes toward the middle of the first half. He received a ball, controlled it, and took a shot on goal. It was right on Canela's chest. He made an attempt to grab it, but the shot was so violent that it threw Canela backward into the net. With the violence of the shot, Canela somehow got knocked out and was taken to a local hospital. Neno didn't know how to replace Canela because most of the guys were scared, so they took turns. Whenever the fat fellow shot, it went right in because the guys were afraid of him. So the score was 12 to 0, with the fat player scoring seven of the twelve. This situation seldom occurs, but never underestimate players due to their appearance. My good friend Ezio had a leg that was shorter than the other one but was able to run and play the inside left like very few people could. Not only was he able to take control of the game, but also he was able to deliver excellent shots on goal. He was always a starting player on every team he played for.

Neno was a mild-mannered man who did a lot of training himself. He was in shape, but not too many people were interested in taking him into a fight. The times that I had seen him in fights, he completely demolished the opponents using head butts and kicks with punches as a follow-up. He didn't have too many enemies.

The second coach was a gentleman who came from Yugoslavia. His name was Mr. Glizowycz. He was brought to the US to coach the Ukrainian Nationals of Philadelphia. He was an older man, perhaps fifty years old or older. We had a very good team in Philadelphia, and I was playing inside left. During various practices, he noticed that I was dribbling too much. After one of the games, he told me that if I wanted to continue with the team, I would have to dribble less and pass more. I think that was in '60s season. I loved soccer, so I started to worry about my playing position. I started passing the ball more frequently. That year, I was invited to play in Canada for the Toronto Roma SC, and I progressed into an incredible passer.

My game improved a lot because I had a feel for the ball. So that season, I played mostly a one-touch game, and I did very well. We won the Canadian championship. The middle field were Gordon Bradley, Sanchez Garcia, and me. I took the place of an international player from Peru by the name of Cubillas. Gordon Bradley coached New York Cosmos when Pelé was playing. Sanchez Garcia was later signed by the Philadelphia Ukrainians, helping them bring a couple of Unites States championships. It was a great season for Toronto Roma. In the final game, we beat Toronto Italia 1 to 0 in the Varsity stadium with a crowd of about twenty thousand people. Most of our success came from our middle field, who defended and attacked constantly. Gordon Bradley was strong and objective. Sanchez Garcia was highly technical, and I contributed with my passing and pushing our team to a defensive mode. I believe that I helped a lot to win that particular game.

The third coach I respected was Geza Henni, who coached the US World Cup Team in 1965. We played against Mexico in LA. We were leading 2 to 1 with less than a minute to go when our goaltender, Victor Gerley, had possession of the ball and a Mexican forward named Padilla, in desperation, attacked him with his chest. He got upset and threw the ball at the Mexican forward's head when Victor already had possession of the ball. The referee was running back to the middle field, looking at his watch to end the game. That event caused him to call a penalty shot. Consequently, the game ended in a tie. We then went to Mexico the following day, which was a Friday, and practice was set for Saturday morning. The game was set to be played on Sunday at noon in Mexico City at Ciudad Universitaria stadium. We were in the hands of Geza's assistant coach and physical trainer, George Mayer. I was exhausted from playing the game in LA, and frankly, I needed a rest before the game on Sunday; but Geza had an assistant who decided to give us a hard practice on Saturday morning. I was still hurting from the previous game so I requested to rest when the assistance coach said, "If you don't practice, then you don't play!" Geza had gone to Central America to see our next adversary. I felt that I couldn't handle both the practice and the game. So I did not practice, and consequently, I did not expect to play on Sunday.

When Geza came back, he had a Sunday morning meeting and discussed the game and the lineup. Geza went on delegating the starters, their positions, and instructions. He went to passing my number 6, so I understood the situation and felt okay with the bench. He passed by numbers 7, 8, and 9, and then he mentioned my name for 10. I was shocked because 10 was Walt Chyzowych's number. He was already upset because he didn't play in Los Angeles. I never worried about things like that, but the coach made the decision so I was there to cover his command. Walt voiced his complaint, but the coach decided to go his way regardless. I felt somewhat unhappy because this provoked an undesirable situation between Walt, Coach Geza, and me. We lost that game 2 to 0. We had two goals cancelled by the referee due to his judgment. In my evaluation, one of the goals was legitimate.

After the game, we had another meeting in which Walt told the coach that since we lost, there was no need to take me to Honduras so that he could therefore play in my place. When I heard about that conversation, I also became upset. How could a player address the coach in that way? I appreciated Coach Geza's attitude for asking me if I wanted to go to Honduras as I was already scheduled to play. I thought about that incoherent behavior and decided to go back to the University of Maryland because we were having exams at that time. That gave Walt his opportunity to play in the World Cup competition. I felt disappointed because nobody would feel good placed in that ridiculous situation, but it was just that I was trying to help people. In fact, there was never a situation in my life that I didn't try to help people. Nobody would help me if I were in a situation similar to that. So Walt eventually became coach of a college in the USA. I think that he also blamed me for what happened on that day, always cutting my wings for the possibility of coaching in a major college in the USA. This event precipitated my return to Brazil in 1965.

To top this event, I was selected by the US federation as the best player of the year. A banquet was given in my honor at the Schwarzwald Inn in Philadelphia where I gave a speech declining to play in future US games due to what happened in the previous two World Cup games. It was a terrible decision because I was only twenty-five years old and in my best shape ever.

It was after these two World Cup games that I decided to go back to Brazil. I had gotten married and wanted to live with my wife, and my first baby was already on the way. I really can't blame anyone but myself. I was in love and became very sensitive to everything around me. I had nobody to ask for advice, so I made my own decisions.

So these three coaches were the ones whom I can remember well. However, there was another person who helped me with my soccer playing, and that was Lajos Varga. He came to America from Hungary in the late fifties and was an excellent player as well as a very nice person. He was playing for the Ukrainian nationals when I met him. He spent time trying to teach me some of the Hungarian ways of the game. He was a middle fielder and knew a lot about the position. His teachings helped me to become a better player. Lajos really loved soccer. He was a short man, but he played some incredible games. He became a pro coach and was greatly respected wherever he played or coached.

CHAPTER FOUR

In the fifties, I was in my early teens surviving my past ordeals with soccer. My neighborhood in Brazil began to grow, and a new men's soccer team began to flourish. The Brazilian people really love soccer. There were always club arguments. So every person there had a team they rooted for. Somehow that becomes like a religion, an extreme desire to have your team win no matter how, and could be honest or dishonest as long as you are on top. For many people, a loss was like losing the war or something extremely important for each individual. These matters were for clubs; now imagine when the national team played. It was like a holiday. Schools would close, most businesses would close, and the people cared about the game more than anything else. I remember having classes in the evening when the Brazil national team played. I came from a school that was open in the afternoon, expecting to teach at night in another school. It was dark; there were no lights anywhere in the building, so I went home to see the game like everyone else. They had many soccer holidays, especially when the World Cup games were being played or if there was a celebration related to an important win.

In Brazil, they allow young kids to play up to eighteen years of age before considering professionalism. It was unusual for younger kids to play for what they called *esporte* (a soccer team of adults), which dealt with adult soccer. Most of the players who played in Neno's team were playing on men's teams. I was one of the boys.

I was fifteen years old when I played four full games every weekend. The main team was called "Metropolitano," for whom I played on Sunday afternoons. We played on our own field, and there were most of my União teammates. We grew up playing together. Most of the kids were of the same age, except we were all playing in the *esporte* team. In this setup, I did learn a lot about soccer by playing four games a week and by watching better players to learn some new moves.

Playing in the Unites States is so different because the kids don't have their heroes in front of them. Therefore, they somewhat play rustic soccer. When in Brazil, one refines his play; in the US, they make you hustle, and no emphasis is put on dribbles or skills such as ball control. While in Brazil, I watched Djalma Santos, a World Cup player, squeeze the ball from one foot to the other, raising the ball as high as his chest on plays on a number of occasions throughout the game. I decided to try it in the US, and I did it in games when I received the ball and was unmarked. I would bring the ball up while running, and not one of our players were able to do it.

Some of the players in the four clubs where I played in Brazil were extremely good at some quality or another. So I practiced to get better with the samba rhythm following my steps. It was very important to be a starter on any of those four teams. They had fans who came every Sunday to watch them. After each game, there was a little celebration in which the fans and the players got together to talk about the game. The people who followed these teams were almost as fanatical as the ones who followed the pros. So when there was any altercation, teams fought against the other neighborhoods. It was like a war in the making whenever we played each other. Some of the rivalry would cause fights, and many times the players and fans were seriously injured. On one occasion, we were playing an army team, and we basically won it. But no one messed with the army! They came back with trucks loaded with soldiers and beat up anyone they could find. In fact, one of our players got caught alone in the street and was severely beat up. No police came because they were dealing with the army. Nobody messes with the army in Brazil.

Some players whom I can remember helped me achieve better playing qualities. I remember a player whose name was Israel; he was a light mulatto with great skills. He had moves quite unseen around our way. There was another middle-aged player whose nickname was "Cabeleira," which means a lot of hair. His feet were as smooth as his hands. He had tremendous ball control and fantastic ball protection. There was another young man named Miquiba, a fantastic dribbler. Lalo was another middle fielder who had tremendous ball control and fantastic dribbles. Among these guys, you can't help but learn and later apply these moves on games when you become confident and able to do them. We had one player by the name of Ze Gordo who was a very intelligent guy. He, together with Neno and another local named Jorge who studied to be a medical doctor, managed to rob the Caixa Economica Bank by having Jorge go in the bank to see a friend; and when his friend left his desk, he punched assets into one of their names. So during lunch, Ze Gordo would go to the bank and withdraw incredible amounts of money. That was done more for fun than for need. Then Ze Gordo would go back to the neighborhood, rent two or three taxis, and take all of his friends to Santos to eat and drink it up for free. For them it was a great time. This bank was federal, so they were committing a federal crime. When they got caught, they went to federal prison for a few months and were later released. Ze Gordo was the first player I saw trapping the ball from the air with the face of his foot.

One Sunday afternoon, we went to play at a place called Vinhedo Terra do Vinho (vineland). They had regular stadium, and as the game went on, one of their players kicked the ball high in the air. When the ball came down, Ze Gordo trapped it with the face of his foot, making the ball dead on the spot. The referee stopped the game. He wanted to check the ball whether it was full of air or empty. He soon verified that the ball was full of air. Thus, the game continued on until there was a fight because of that strange incident. We had to run away to the train station to catch the first train available. We were all scared of what these people from the "interior" country could do to us. They were holding big weed-clipping knives or country tools to do their justice on us. Somehow we all got on the train, leaving their threats behind.

Three of the clubs I played for were from our neighborhood. The outside club was called Estrela do Moinho Velho (Star of the Old Windmill). They were stronger than our local teams, and it took me a while to get used to their game until eventually they started me on their first team. Those guys played very good games and also partied hard after most of them. One day, we were all invited for lunch and our goalie, Negrao, cooked for all of us. Everyone got a platter of rice, beans, and meat. After everyone ate, someone thought of asking what kind of meat it was. Negrao told them it was cat meat. Most of the guys got sick and were trying to throw up. I felt somewhat sick but couldn't throw up. I enjoyed it while I was eating it so . . . what? Every so often, some player or fan would pull tricks on us, for fun of course. While Neno worked in the post office, he founded a team to play on Saturday afternoons. He invited most of the União players, which included Ze Gordo and me. There was another player named Motofeno, who was a good ballplayer and also a tenor singer. He knew some Italian opera songs and would entertain us along the way. Ze Gordo was also an entertainer and would tell us jokes, and he played *pandeiro* (small drums specially made in Brazil) like a professional.

One Saturday, afternoon we went to play in the interior (inland, out of town). We took a train ride for an hour and a half then played a hard game and tried. On the way back, there was a forbidden area at the railroad station so I somehow went inside of it. The police were called, and I was arrested; but we had a cop on the team, Motofeno, who said he would take me in. He was wearing his uniform as we got on the train that was about to leave; they realized the cop took me into the train. As soon as he got me on the train, he changed his police uniform and dressed with the team uniform and put a different hat on his head and made believe we were asleep on the train. From where we were, the train stopped at every station until it reached São Paulo; we left the station and went back to the post office. Then we were all hungry, so we went to a restaurant not far from the post office. We were about ten players and took up several tables. Then the music started with the usual entertainers, Motofeno and Ze Gordo. After several hours, we left the restaurant, and on the way out, Ze Gordo got a hold of one of the beautiful jackets that was hanging on one of the hangers and put it on and walked out with no intimidation. He found some money inside the jacket, which he spent on drinks for everyone later.

In the meantime, I had started working in downtown São Paulo as a delivery boy for Mr. DeBoer. One afternoon, I saw a stranger in the office. He was looking around and had a meeting with Mr. DeBoer. Later, he found out that there were some checks missing, so we were all invited to his head table and questioned. Of course, most of the guilt was pointed toward me. I felt really embarrassed because I never stole anything from anyone. After investigating further, they finally realized that it might have been this man from Argentina who could have taken the checks. Mr. DeBoer excused himself for a few minutes, saying that he had to go into the darkroom to verify some film development. He had a detective there disguised as a worker, waiting to arrest the man if he was found guilty. After ten minutes, he came out of the darkroom, catching the guy in the act. He then put the check in his mouth and was going to swallow it. The detective came in and punched him in the stomach, making him spit the check back out. From there, the detective took him to jail, and my name was clean again.

In order to prove that you are honest, you sometimes have to go through these events. Sometimes you will get caught and pay for what someone else did, unless you prove your innocence. My life had some of these events that helped strengthen my character and fortitude. It is my belief that experience helps many people make good decisions. I still made my share of mistakes.

CHAPTER FIVE

When I was seventeen, I was reasonably established as a good soccer player in my neighborhood. I never thought of becoming a professional ballplayer. In Brazil, the competition was great; but like any sport, you need someone to connect you to the right people. Many different fans told me that they were connected and that they would recommend me, but it never happened. My mother was a US citizen, and she was trying to get me to join the navy in the US. She never perceived that I would need special training in the English language. I spoke a little German because that was the language my parents used around the house. I had learned how to speak Portuguese fluently, but I hardly spoke any English. Her dream was that I would become a captain in the US Navy. That was not my dream although I wanted to please her. She had gone through a lot of hardship leaving Germany in the late 1920s and going to the USA. She was a beautiful young German woman. In the United States, she worked as a maid for rich people. Later, she got married to my father in Atlantic City; and she, my father, her sister, and her sister's husband went to California where she worked as a cook for a movie star.

When the time for me to come to the United States was approaching, I felt very uneasy. I was used to life in Brazil. I felt that many of my dreams would never come true. I was just surviving. I worked during the day and went to school at night to complete high school. So in 1955, I graduated from *ginasio* (junior high school) in Brazil. I remember it well; it was also the first time I got upset for catching my sister with a boy. My gang and I followed her and caught this guy, and it was not very pleasant.

In 1956, my father's bar and store were open, selling food and drinks. The day came when my father had to travel to Santos to get my tickets to travel to the USA. I came home earlier than usual, around eight in the evening. My mother was taking care of the bar; there was a tall black man who apparently had too much to drink. He started insulting my mother for being German and did not want to pay his bill. The bar was somewhat high off the road; one would need to climb two steps to get to the bar. For us to get to our house, we would need to climb an extra ten steps to reach the living room. I came home and saw this commotion going on and the blatant disrespect for my mother, so I went upstairs and she came after me, begging me not to do anything that I would later regret. Then I heard him calling her a dirty German and other unpleasant curse words. I was upstairs, listening, until the point that I couldn't stand it anymore. I waited until he approached the front door and the bigger step. I came running down the steps, and when he turned to see what was going on, I flew with my two feet and hit him in the chest. With my impulse and his surprise, he went flying out of the bar over the steps, landing outside near a mud puddle. I wound up on top of him, pushing his face into the mud puddle, punching him at will. He managed to get up slowly and promised to return to make me pay for what I had just done. He walked up to Vergueiro Street, where he met some of his friends and convinced them to come with him and get me. About an hour later, they came back to our bar. I was at the door, waiting for his gang. Some of the guys from the group recognized me for my soccer ability, and they greeted me, apologizing, and turned around and beat that man again. This time, he really got some injuries. I guess he forgot the idea of getting even with me. This incident happened while my father was in Santos buying the ticket for me to go to the USA. I felt really good for being able to defend my mother in such a gallant way. My father was also very pleased with me.

My mother and I went downtown to shop for clothes to take on my trip. The days were drawing short. My father got his truck to take me to Santos to embark on a Norwegian ship to the US.

It was a smaller-size ship. I had never traveled a long time by ship or by plane. It was all new to me. The day came in July, and the weather was nice. I began to feel uneasy. The idea of being away from my parents hadn't quite sunk in. I said goodbye to my parents and boarded the ship with a heavy suitcase. As the ship left the port, I was losing sight of my parents. I never felt so alone in my life; I was seventeen years old and being sent out to face the world. With profound tears in my eyes, I watched my parents and siblings disappear in the horizon. It was like being ripped apart. I shall never forget that trip. The smaller ship went from Santos to Rio de Janeiro, from Rio to Recife in the Northeast Brazil, then to Philadelphia, and finally to New York. We couldn't get off the ship in Philadelphia because of customs, so I had to wait an extra day to get to New York. From New York, I came to Philadelphia by bus and finally a taxi to get to my Uncle Gustav and Aunt Louisle in Philadelphia.

While in Rio, I went to the Corcovado Mountain where the statue of Jesus was looking at us. This was one of the toughest trips I ever took. In the middle of it, the sea began to get rough and the waves grew bigger, splashing against the ship to the point that the ship would go totally under them. I was in a metallic room with my body going up and down on a metallic bed. I really became afraid; I couldn't sleep. Then the ship continued fighting this strange battle against the raging sea. The next day, the sea was calm and the sun appeared radiantly in the sky. Although the meals were very well prepared, I was seasick and had a hard time eating. Every meal was complete with some type of seafood. By the time I got to Philadelphia, I must have lost at least ten pounds. My cheeks were sunken in. I felt so happy to put my feet on solid ground again. For the first time in my life, I saw New York's skyline and the Statue of Liberty. I had no idea if soccer even existed in the USA. When my uncle took me to a German club in Philadelphia, that was the first time I saw soccer in the USA.

CHAPTER SIX

My objective of coming to the USA had nothing to do with soccer. I loved the game because of my background in Brazil. I missed it a lot, but I intended to join the navy as my mother wished. I was informed of a place for registration for the military near Erie Avenue in Philadelphia. I went there and found out where and how to register for the navy. At that time, my English was very poor; I couldn't speak it or write it. They gave me some elementary tests to identify some objects on a paper. I had no idea what they were asking of me, so I failed miserably. I began to live with my uncle and got myself a job at Bryn Athyn Cathedral.

One Sunday, my uncle took me to a German club called Erzgebirge, and there was a soccer game being played. I enjoyed watching, and during a break, I got a hold of a ball and started playing with it. Some people saw me and asked me to join their team. It was a third division team in the United Soccer League of Pennsylvania. I immediately joined. Nobody knew me except that I was a child of German parents. I spoke enough German to understand what was going on. We had two practices a week and a game on Sundays. I turned eighteen and forgot about the idea of joining the navy. I had no idea what I was doing there, especially since I was shy by nature. I only spoke when spoken to. But as soon as people saw me playing on Sundays, I made some friends.

It was hard to adapt from playing four *esporte* games in Brazil to playing one game a week in a different temperature. In the fall, we had nice days; but when we reached the winter, we played a lot less when the weather was unbearable. Of course, being alone in America wasn't easy. In Brazil, I had a girlfriend and we were quite close, but here in this frigid weather with no women around, it was difficult to survive.

I missed my family's warmth, with my brother and sisters being alive in my heart and my mother and father especially. I felt like moving back to Brazil. I made friends with some of the players who were seniors in high school. I envied them because I couldn't share school with them; instead, I had to work to make a living. I started to become comfortable in that lifestyle. On holidays on weekends, I used to take really long walks and run around the area to keep in shape. I missed my samba school in Brazil. How could you explain such a thing to the people living here in America?

I became friends with a young kid named Alfred. We played soccer together. We met at practices and weekends during the games. He came from Romania and had a German background. He had his parents around. Although I had my aunt and uncle, whom I respected greatly, it was not the same. One Saturday, we were walking north on Fifth Street in Philadelphia when some kids from the neighborhood were around harassing people. They started bothering Alfred and I in front of Incarnation Church. Then they disappeared, so Alfred and I started walking toward Rockland Street. Before we reached the next block, the gang came toward us. They were intending to jump at us. They grabbed Alfred and punched him; I was about thirty yards away. Alfred defended himself by punching them back then the other gang members started jumping on him, kicking and punching. When I saw what was going on, I came back running and sideswiped the first guy so he whirled around and landed on top of a car that stopped there due to the brawl. He landed with his head next to the car's bumper. I came running and kicked his head against the bumper. Then I went to help Alfred who was trying to fight four kids. I took one and gave him a head butt and a sideswipe, and he was on the ground, and Alfred was able to take care of the others. In the meantime, someone had called the cops. They came quickly and arrested all of us. Some lady was watching from her window and saw how the fight had started. She came to the Thirty-fifth District to testify on behalf of Alfred and I. So they released us. The kids who fought with us were detained, and because they were belligerent, they got in trouble with one of the detectives who invited one of the tougher boys into a room. Leaving the door slightly open, this kid had sideburns down his cheeks, trying to carry on Elvis's style. The detective asked him to hit him like he was hitting us and the kids with the bike. They had stolen the kid's bike and had given him a beating earlier. Luckily, Alfred and I were better able to defend ourselves; otherwise, we would have taken a beating. The detective then proceeded to give that kid a beating until he was taken to the hospital. Alfred's parents came and blamed me for the event. He was forbidden to hang out with me, but our friendship still continues today. I wasn't guilty of anything except helping my friend in trouble at that particular time. So it was easy for them to find me guilty, mostly because I came from South America. Some Europeans at that time were very prejudiced against us South Americans.

I acquired a mixture of cultures that helped me endure some of the difficult times in my life. As I played for Erzgebirge, I began to find my identity. They treated me well, and I participated in many of their social events. I could feel that I was unwanted by some of these people because I wasn't one of them. I was brought up totally different than they were. At eighteen, I was already a man, whereas in the USA, at eighteen, most kids were totally dependent on their families. I felt alone and embarrassed while the other kids were having a ball. To be alone in a foreign country is very depressing and lonely. I was a relatively good-looking boy, and I'm sure many girls wished to be my companion; but I was alienated because I didn't grow up like them, I didn't go to school like them, and I wasn't like them.

CHAPTER SEVEN

In 1956, playing for Erzgebirge was a lot of fun for me. We played for enjoyment, and I was slowly learning what America was all about. Working at Bryn Athyn Cathedral, I was learning the trade of cabinet making. We did woodwork around the church building and around the castles of Mr. Raymond Pitcairn. No nails were used in that church. They were among the richest people in America. They founded that church using Emanuel Swedenbourg, a Swedish philosopher as their guide. Being a Catholic, I did not join that religion, but I had great respect for it. The grounds around the cathedral were of an imposing beauty. On sunny days, the gardens were breathtaking. My father had worked for these people during his stay in the United States. So I was recommended by my father's friend, Mr. Paul Schmitz, and they accepted me with no problem. My biggest problem was when my sister drowned while swimming in the ocean in Santos by the shore in Brazil. My immediate boss, Rudy, told me if I left the country, I would lose my job. For an event like this, I would have to go back regardless of Rudy's opinion. I went to Mr. Pitcairn and explained my situation. He told me to look him up upon my return.

This was a severe blow to my parents, having one daughter dead and I away from home. I loved my sister, and I was really shocked. Consequently, I went back to Brazil and spent three months with my parents. I came back to America and went to see Mr. Pitcairn. He sent me to his son, Garth, who gave me a job in the winter of 1958. I had to start cars at the used car lot, wash them every day, and make deliveries of the repaired cars from the mechanical shop.

I loved to ride those new Imperials. Inside of them, I felt like a millionaire. Normally, I would speed them through Route 1 and use some of the time to have breakfast. One day I was having breakfast at the diner, and I didn't notice two policemen having breakfast there as well. As I left the diner, I spun the wheels. The policemen came and followed me until I got into the shop's garage. They just followed me, and instead of talking to me, they went to Mr. Garth Pitcairn while I looked on surprised to see them having a pleasant conversation. I kind of realized that I was going to get fired, so I talked to my boss about resigning. He actually wasn't going to fire me, but since I brought it up, it just ended right there. I was looking forward to the tryouts for the Olympics in St. Louis the following month.

While all of this was happening in 1958, the people of Erzgebirge were talking about moving me to the major division. Mr. Binkele was the coach; he thought I was not strong enough. They played more roughly in the majors. Their major division team had players like Walt Bahr, Pete Kennedy, Benny McLaughlan, and many other famous local players from time to time. I was a stranger, and many of them didn't care about me either way. They talked and discussed enough, and I was the cause of it. Their decision came down that I wasn't strong or tall enough to play major division ball. Either I'd continue playing third division or I would have to quit the club.

At the end of 1957, there was talk about the Ukrainians entering the professional league. I decided to go out for it. From the beginning, they never criticized me about my size. I came to their practices and met many of their players. Among them were Walt and Gene Chyzowycz, Lajos Varga, Paul Varga, Walter Harosym, Andy Raez, Walter Kudenko, Charlie Garcia, George Kuluchenko (goalie), and Harry Levy. They seemed satisfied with my abilities at the time, but I seldom played. I was a substitute for Alex Falk, their main goal scorer. I never minded sitting on the bench. It was good for me; they paid me, and I was with a good team. Those days, Walt and Gene Chyzowycz were starters. I came in as a forward, as an inside left. In those days, we played the WM format; and as time went on, the team changed formations. I started playing as a defensive halfback. That was where I felt more comfortable while I was playing for the United Soccer League.

O brasileiro, de Mogi das Cruzes, Alexandre Ely ...

Brasileiro dá aulas de football na Filadélfia - Estados Unidos

Nascido em Mogi das Cruzes, o jovem Ely ensina o esporte das multidões aos americanos na University Maryland ---- E' medio volante do Ukrainian Nationals da Philadelfia que disputa o campeonato da Liga Profissional do Este dos EE.UU. — Está visitando a familia em São Paulo --- Vai levar técnico e jogadores brasileiros para o seu club — Aviso aos descendentes de ucranianos

.... WANDERLEY LOPES   Foto de RUBENS BOCCIA)

I had the opportunity of playing in a forward line whenever Alex Falk was hurt or couldn't play due to injuries. One day, we had an important game against New York, and the coach played me half a game. I started getting more playing time because Alex Falk scored less, and I started scoring more. The club received notice to send their US citizens to St. Louis for a tryout for the US Pan American and Olympic team. Unfortunately, there were only three United States citizens on the team. They were I, Walter Kudenko, and George Kuluchenko (goalie). On the Saturday night prior to our trip, Walter Kudenko had a car accident and was almost killed. Walter was an excellent fullback; he was good defensively and excellent offensively at the same time. If he were in St. Louis, he would definitely have made the team. Due to that accident, only the two of us were left and went—Kuluchenko and myself. Soon I became a starter in the Ukes, but I was given this fantastic opportunity to be selected for the US Pan American Games in 1959. All of this came together as I quit Mr. Pitcairn's job, enabling me to travel to the US trials in St. Louis.

Alexandre Ely dá "show" de bola nos Estados Unidos.

At that time, Hungary had become free from communism and many Hungarians had fled to the USA. At the Ukes, we had a large group—Lajos and Paul Varga, Bela Zahar, Andy Racz, and Tony Domboroski. They were all fairly good ballplayers.

During the US tryout, the selecting managers made four different teams. They were divided into north, south, east, and west. They played each other, and I was placed on the weakest team. I didn't play as well as I could have because I had a cast on from a broken collarbone. In a game against the Kensington Blue Bells team, I had obtained that serious injury. I was taken to a hospital and left there for treatment for a broken collarbone. Nobody came to see me to find out how I was feeling as I lay in the hospital, wondering about my future. The only person who came to visit me was a young Ukrainian girl. Her name was Zenya. She gave me hopes that there were some people who cared out there but couldn't come to visit me. It was a painful experience to be injured in a situation like that. I was not happy when I finally got out of the hospital. I had no money. Thank God for the Ukrainian family of Walter Meducha that gave me one good meal a day that kept me healthy.

Traveling back from the St. Louis tryouts, we were listening to the news to find out which players were selected. They picked eighteen players and two alternates; I was the last player they picked. My name was there in case some player could not make the Pan American games in Chicago in 1959. I really didn't count on being able to play. My mail was received on the weekends when I came to Philadelphia to practice indoor in the winter and outdoor in the fall and spring. Our games were always on Sunday, home or away. I started receiving mail from the Pan American Games. I couldn't believe it until I finally got the airline tickets to travel to Chicago in the summer of 1959.

CHAPTER EIGHT

Pan American Games (Chicago, 1959)

had recently taken the cast off my chest from a broken collarbone. Besides being shy and quiet, I made friends quicker than most because I seldom got into unpleasant conversations with my teammates or outsiders. The player's name that had broken my collarbone was Wally Porter, a very strong player from the Kensington Blue Bells. They were a tough team to beat. It was on an Open Cup game, which we won, but they were a very violent team. Wally and I became friends because he couldn't believe that I went after him in the game after he fouled me.

Most of us were single, and in our spare time, we would go to clubs in Philadelphia. One night at one of those clubs, I was ordering my drink, I didn't know that Wally was there. I was facing a mirror when he approached me from behind and grabbed me by the neck. I thought my time had come. He let me go and started telling me that he couldn't believe that I came back after him on the field. The ball was pushed between us, and Wally had one step on me. I went after him and gave him one of those *rasteira* kicks that made him fall and get injured. I was definitely hurting when I came back on the field. They were one of the roughest teams I ever played in my life thus far, and I felt it with my injuries. During the time I played soccer in Brazil, I seldom was hurt. Here in the States, from the time I played for Erzgebirge to the Ukrainians, I would need a warm bath after the games to sooth my aching legs. They were beat up so badly that it seemed like my legs were trampled by a bunch of wild horses. The soccer I played was mostly of a South American–style player.

In the beginning of the summer of 1959, I started believing that I wasn't dreaming when I finally received airline tickets with directions where to go. We arrived in Chicago from different parts of the United States. We were there at least two weeks prior to our first real game. They first gave us a complete uniform with two shirts and a flag-colored hat for the parade in Soldier Field. That was like a dream to me that was finally coming true.

Chicago Parade

USA (1960)

During the introductory parade, the soccer team was all dressed up in blue jackets and gray pants with white shoes, including the colorful hat. We looked great. This was a very unique experience. As we came close to the end, I noticed all the South and Central American countries represented in the parade. There were great moments, but that moment as the US national anthem played in the background, it really shook me up. I had just returned from South America due to my sister's death, and this emotion really caught me unprepared. After the parade, I went out of the playing area and went to the stands. That was where I met Miss America. She was very beautiful. I spoke to her in my broken English, trying to get a date, but I don't think we could understand each other to get anything going. What a shame! At night, we were invited to a dinner offered by the city in which we met all of the ambassadors from all of the countries that were present. Then I met two beautiful girls. One was the daughter of the Mexican ambassador, and the other was the sister of the Costa Rican ambassador. The Mexican girl's name was Carmen, and the Costa Rican girl was Aziadee. I dated both of them. With Carmen, I even lost a car that I had borrowed from a friend in Chicago.

Alex Ely with Miss America

Being the youngest player, I knew by the lineup that my chances of playing were slim. My main idea was to enjoy all that was given to me and make the most of it. I just came from Brazil with nothing, and I was ready to play against them even if I wasn't a starter. Our coach was Jimmy Reid, an older man from Rutgers University. We were not the favorites by a long shot. We started our preparation by playing a few exhibition games. We played Indiana University right outside of Chicago. For this first game, I was a reserve player. I enjoyed watching our team play against a very tough team. That resulted in one of the halfbacks breaking his leg. He was a good player so that was not the best of news for us. He was in his late twenties and experienced. His name was John Traina. He was done for the games. His immediate substitute was Val Pelizzaro. I kept on practicing and hoping for chance if it would ever come.

The next game was against Chicago Schwaben, a strong amateur team from the area. This game the starter was Val Pelizzaro. It was summertime in Chicago, and the heat was intense. Toward the beginning of the second half, Val got overheated; and for the first time, I was called to enter an official game. That game earned me a starting position on the team. Now the real games were on. The first game was against Argentina. We were totally overwhelmed by the *gringos* (word used by Brazilians to describe Argentinians). They beat us 4 to 1. The second game was against Brazil. The players and I got together for a meeting. We had a good group of players, but some realized that we would have to play a hell of a lot better and make plans so that we wouldn't get surprised like we were with Argentina. We had two outstanding players in the forward line, Edward Murphy and Al Zerhusen. They were among the highest scorers in the tournament.

USA Pan American Team (1959)

In the United States Olympic book, they mentioned the loss to Costa Rica. What really happened was that I played against Cuba a few days before and got injured. One of the Cuban players kicked me on the left side of my ankle, causing a wound that was tough to heal. The wax from the Cuban player's shoe was what caused my infection. The doctors and trainers did their best to get me able to play, but I was just not well enough at that point. My name appeared in the 1960 Olympic Book as being "particularly tough to take as Alex Ely was unable to play and Costa Rica had a four to two lead at half time." Even with me, the US returned strong in the second half and pressured Costa Rica, with balls hitting the goalpost and the goalie making miraculous defenses. It was just bad luck that kept us away from a silver medal. We wound up earning the bronze instead. I believe that was the first medal the US had earned in soccer at the time. We had a friendly, talented group that really deserved to make that team. We had an excellent goaltender, Victor Otoboni. Joe Speca knew me from playing against him in our league. He played for the Baltimore Pompei, and they had a very competitive team at that time. Zenon Snylyk was our captain. A well-educated man and a good player, he was somewhat arrogant due to our cultural differences. When playing against Spanish teams, I was his interpreter. He was a Ukrainian who became a college professor. We were as different as day and night. We had a very strong player from New York, Gene Grabrowski. George Brown got hurt at the beginning games. He was a great player and also a great friend of mine. During the game against Brazil, Gene's job was to mark Gerson, who later became a famous player in the world of soccer. I told Gene the only way to mark him was to stay close and divide the balls and also to hit hard when and if the opportunity came. Gene got Gerson carried off the field on a divided play, and I believe that sort of helped us win that game. This all happened in the first half. Our forward line was aggressive and dangerous. A couple of goals came from my crossing the ball to Murphy's head. Al Zerhusen had a couple, and Bill Loobe had one. I had only dreamt about playing soccer in stadiums, and now I was actually doing it against Brazil.

After beating Brazil, we played Haiti. They were basically good players with the ball, but when they got near our goal, they wasted shots. They played good individual soccer but as a team left a lot to be desired. We played objective soccer. With three passes, we were in front of their net. The difference was that we didn't miss as many goals as they did. Anyone watching that game would have the impression that they were winning. The score was 7 to 2 for the US.

With Mexico, we were the better team all around. They just couldn't break our defense lines, and we produced enough counter-attacks with our dangerous forward line. We won the game, but the score could have been higher because we dominated that game.

PAGINA DOS   MEXICO. D. F.   NOVEDADES

Muy Difícil Para México

ALEX Ely

UNO DE LOS MEJORES JUGADORES QUE TRAE EL TEAM AMATEUR NORTEAMERICANO DE FUTBOL!

ALEX NACIO EN BRASIL, SUS PADRES SON DE E.U. Y EN LA TIERRA CARIOCA PRACTICO EL FUTBOL DESDE LOS SIETE AÑOS

NOS VAMOS A EUROPA!

NUESTROS PRIMOS VIENEN DISPUESTOS A REFRENDAR SU TRIUNFO DE CHICAGO!

Choque de Felinos: Pumas Vs. Tigres

Los "Prin
Dado Sor
se ven mu

Los Nuestros Juga
Condiciones que e
Juegos Panameric
no se Pueden ver (

Por EMILIO ZAX

El encuentro de hoy, a las :
versitaria entre los seleccionade
co y los Estados Unidos buscai
a la próxima olimpiada de Ri
nuestros chamacos, debido al bi
el once norteamericano que tan
do sobre el césped, antes y e
vos Panamericanos celebrados i
humillaron a los brasileños.

Claro que los integrantes del
seleccionado nacional estarán
en mejores condiciones de pe-
learles el triunfo a los sobri-
nos del Tío Sam, de como se
encontraban en Chicago ahora
en los panamericanos, pues por
principio de cuentas jugarán
ante "su" público en condiciones normales por completo y en
una cancha natural, pues como
se sabe, allá en Chicago salie-
ron agobiados por el calor a
jugar en una cancha de dimen-
siones muy especiales.

En fin, poco falta para saber
el resultado de este encuentro,
en el que no se podrán hacer
cambios de ninguna especie,
por ser un encuentro de elimi-
natoria olímpica.

Ahora, por otra parte, tene-
mos que decir de los "primos",
que muchos de ellos han per-
tenecido a la selección norte-
americana que se ha medido
con la selección profesional
mexicana, y con equipos muy
poderosos, lo que no deja de
darles una supremacía en el
terreno.

Después de este encuentro
no se volverán a ver las caras
sino hasta el 13 de noviembre
próximo en la ciudad de Los
Angeles, Cal., en el último encuentro, para saber cuál de es-
tos equipos es el que se enfren-
te a un sudamericano para ga-
narse el lugar en la olimpiada

I think we were the great surprise of that tournament. That was the first time that I received an invitation from one of the Brazilian coaches to go back to Brazil to play for the Flamengo SC. By being young and inexperienced, I decided to decline the offer. My reasons were that I just came back from Brazil and I wasn't ready to go back to face uncertainty. Some of these requests weren't considered seriously because I was in the decision-making alone. My parents lived in Brazil, and they never saw me playing soccer. The fact that I played for the USA nationally did not mean anything to my parents. I'm quite sure that most of the players had better reasons to play, but I played for myself. They played for the love of their country, and I played for my eternal love of soccer and the love of my new country. Before every game, they played the national anthem for both sides. Against Brazil, it brought tears to my eyes, and it took a while to pull myself together. I just couldn't imagine playing against Brazil. I shall never forget that day and the victory we had that exploded through the US and South America. We were news in the best Brazilian magazines and newspapers. I was in the front page of *Revista dos Esportes* in Brazil. My friends over there couldn't believe that I had come that far in the game. Considering that we basically prepared ourselves for these games when we arrived in Chicago, whereas the other teams seemed to have much longer preparation time. I was also the youngest player on the US team. The other players were from the midtwenties and up. Unfortunately, as I write this book, we have lost Zenon Snelyk, a person who I respected immensely. My bronze medal is still with me, and I will treasure it forever.

UNITED STATES PAN-AMERICAN SOCCER SQUAD

TOP ROW: Ottoboni, Murphy, Ely, Looby, Ganger, Grabowski, Traina, Meyer, trainer.
MIDDLE ROW: Kuleschenko, Palizzaro, Weckle, Schaller, Speca, Zerhusen.
BOTTOM ROW: Brown, Snylyk, Maierhofer, Stachrowsky, Ruscheinski.

WALTER GIESLER, Mgr.

JAMES REED, Coach

CHAPTER NINE

In 1958, at the end of summer, some players were called to go on a trip to Italy with a New York–Italian organization. We were almost finished with our Canadian championship. The manager was De Filipo, a well-known New York promoter. I had no idea what that was all about. We had games scheduled in Cozenza, Naples, and Pescara. The only team I knew was Naples from reading about them in the news. They were playing in the second division in Italy. The team and I were very excited about going overseas. At that time, my sister Irene was living with me in Philadelphia. I had no problems getting my passport because I used to travel back and forth from South America when I would visit my parents. I was playing for Montreal Ukraina, and we were approved for that trip. It was like an all-star team. We had players from Philadelphia, New York, and Canada. Before traveling, I was told to stop in Detroit for the newspapers to take pictures of me and for me to give a radio interview concerning the Open Cup game with Detroit, which was scheduled. Most of the players were actually signed by the teams they were playing for in Canada or in the USA. I was supposed to meet the team in Pescara and join with the other players. In Pescara, I knew a few of the players. Andy Racz from the Ukes in Phila, Bonezzi and Bustamante came along. We all together had more than sixteen players. They played the first game in Pescara before I arrived and lost badly. We had to play Naples, who, after learning about our loss in Pescara, refused to play with us so we were to play the next game with Cozenza.

By that time, most of us were suspended by FIFA because we had left our teams without player's releases to finish their championship. For that game in Cozenza, the manager changed our names to a totally different name. We had to remember our names because if any of us got ejected, the referee would have to put our names on the report. The stadium was full of people, but the Italians were mad at their team, meaning, specifically one ballplayer who was booed since the minute he stepped onto the field. The people did not stop until the coach finally removed the player. The game ended in a tie; it was our best game in that town.

While we were in Pescara, I made some Italian friends. They were very nice; they showed me around their beautiful city. They took me to the sea, and I couldn't help but walk in it. When the water reached my chest, I could look down and see my feet. It was the Mediterranean Sea. My friend, Francesso, introduced me to his family. He had two beautiful sisters. I became friends with one of them. We wrote to each other, but my life as a player continued on. We had very little time to continue our friendship. We went to Rome where I saw the old aqueduct. It is truly amazing what the history in Italy can tell us about past humanity. When I first arrived there, the players were excited about the women. Their women didn't interest me because some of them weren't too clean, and they had their money pimps ready to jump in if they got anyone to pay them.

In the streets of Naples, I got very upset. I've seen these women in daylight. Some were abused, pregnant, and just worn down. It was worse than the situation in Brazil or at least than that of São Paulo. As I was walking in Naples, a young kid came to me, offering me his sister. The kid was fourteen or fifteen years old. He said that his sister was young and pretty, and it would cost me only twenty dollars. I followed the kid until we reached his house. The family was there, and he took me upstairs where his sister was in bed and ready to have sex. I sat by her bed, and she was crying, and that was not the happiest moment of my trip to Italy. I thought of my family and had never come across that kind of misery. The girl was pretty and willing, but

I felt so bad that I couldn't even touch her. I gave her the money and tried to stop her from crying. I could not in any way feel her pain. She became friendly toward me, and I felt friendly also, but the idea of sex was left out. Some of the boys had different plans back at the hotel; there was a prostitute there who was ready to take the whole team. I wasn't interested in that deal. Just the idea of going with a girl after several guys had been with her made me lose my enthusiasm.

These types of incidents happen when teams travel. My personal opinion is to avoid them because they can be costly in many ways. Sometimes it can cost your entire life and career. Some players were married and looked upon that as an opportunity to party away, and only God knows what diseases they could get as a result.

We were actually having fun when we found out that because of game cancellations, there was no money for our return trip. That was a reminder of the day that Mr. Di Felippo gave us our tickets, I never even looked to see what was in the envelope. At that time, I was very naive and trusted people. In reality, that was a big lesson for me. Don't believe in words and don't commit unless you got the proof in your hands. The whole team was terrified; we didn't know what to do. The management promised us tickets in a few days, but they had nothing to give us at the time. I wanted to avenge myself on the manager, but he was a lot smarter than I. He never appeared at any of our meetings or any place we could see him. The end of that tour was sad. Many players had to get money wired for their tickets home. The players who had no money had to wait until management provided them a ticket to return to the US. My sister, Irene, wired me the money for my return ticket. Some of us even went to the US Embassy, and they were unable to help us. Boy, was I glad to be back to the United States after that horrendous but adventurous trip. From that trip, I refused any other invitation to travel with a private team anywhere unless I was sure of the outcome. We went to Italy, but it wasn't as joyous as that kind of trip could have been. In consequence of that trip, we were suspended from FIFA and lost our money and time, learning a lesson that we shall never forget.

CHAPTER TEN

Growing up in Brazil, I had never heard of the Ukraine. I began to know Ukrainians in Philadelphia. Generally speaking, they were mostly hardworking people, very club- and culture-oriented. In 1959, they were struggling to get their independence from Russia. They loved their churches, and their sport was mainly soccer. They decided to build a strong team in Philadelphia. When I first came to their team, most of the players were Ukrainian. They spoke their own language, and I began to grasp words here and there. I was told that some of them spoke German, so I was able to communicate with some of them. They loved their team and used it as a political tool to further their cultural interests. I was young and impressive, so I got to like them and enjoyed many of their cultural customs. The first year we won the US Cup, we brought players from Argentina. They were mostly of Ukrainian descent. The first United States cup was won from the LA Kickers in 1959. They had a very strong team; it took us over three extra overtimes to finally beat them. Mike Noha scored all five goals. I assisted on a few. Mike became like a god to the Ukes. They gave him extra money. Of course, we were all pleased, but Mike took the cake and ate it too. He was a fantastic forward. He obviously took advantage of the situation and demanded a higher pay as he started to slide down to scoring. The team management expected to see him score five goals every game, but they began to see that wasn't going to happen.

In the meantime, we received a visit from the Third Lanark Athletic Club of Scotland. My leg was broken due to a play that Mike Noha started by dribbling and pushed the ball to me on the right side near the outside line, and a player tackled me on an international foul that caused my injury. That was another six months out of the game. Then the team was receiving new players from different parts of the world. To come back from an injury was always very difficult because of fear for hurting yourself again. I couldn't jump right back in. I had to break myself in by playing a little every game until I was able to play a full game again. Some of the Ukrainian players were not happy to see me going to play for the US team. So some of them were denying me passes or trying to set me up on bad plays. I avoided that by practicing hard every week in Maryland. Since I lived there at the university, I had all the facilities around me. Since I played mid-field, I was always with the ball. That made my enemies really upset. Sometimes they would scream my name near the public to push the blame on me for any failure in the defense. I never minded their disparaging attitudes. I always played with my heart in the game; in fact, I always tried to help any new player or anyone who was having trouble with their game. I think that my positive attitude eliminated whatever evil was there, and there was plenty of that around.

Mr. Cox, a millionaire from New York, was sponsoring the American International League in New York. Four players from the Ukrainians were invited, including me, Mike Noha, and three Argentinians named Kravets, Sanchez, and Yacovino. Mike was hurt in a previous game. I advised him not to play; however, he insisted, saying that the *gringos* were too stupid to notice that he was hurt. So he went on playing, and his injury got worse. Eventually he was unable to play. Argentinians referred to Americans as gringos. Consequently, Mike was sold to the Chicago Lyons right after the new International League finished. After losing Mike, Sanchez and I continued playing. We played against the Inter of Milan; there we lost, but someone told us that Ricardo Montalban and Gina Lolobrigida were in the stands watching the game, and Ricardo said that he enjoyed my game. I was very thrilled with that information because all I knew of these two movie stars were from the movies I watched.

The game I best remember was against Nice of France where I missed two open-net sure shots. One went out, and the other one hit the post. That league was interesting because Mr. Cox brought teams from Portugal, France, Italy, and Germany. That brought many fans to Randall Island Stadium to root for their favorite team. New York was able to get a good soccer crowd if the game was important. It is indeed an international city, and there were people from all over the world. I believe that their international league brought success to soccer in New York's area.

I was only twenty years old when VFB Struttgart came to Philadelphia. They were the team from my mother's town, but I was injured at the time and couldn't play. The Ukes lost 3 to 1. The game was quite interesting because we had a player from Argentina by the name of Harry Nunes, whom the Ukes called Harry Niss. He was a great player, yet he couldn't change the result of the game on that day. He was really better than most on the field. Unfortunately, the Ukes lost him. He went back to Argentina. After winning the league games, we went to play the United Scotts of Los Angeles in the finals in 1961. We went to LA with a full team, but the Ukes received news that Mike Noha was coming to play from Argentina; and he did, but he wasn't able to perform that well. In a final game, that was the craziest thing to do. Taking a steady player out to put Michael Noha in was one of the mistakes that they made. The player they took out was a Brazilian player that came from Europe. His name was Casimiro Marin. This player was in excellent shape and knew every phase of the game. When he played, you saw a difference in the style and his passes were like magic. He had scored two beautiful goals in Philadelphia. He kicked a penalty shot by staying very close to the ball since he could shoot with both feet. He normally would hit it and turn to walk toward midfield, knowing that the ball went in. He also helped me to take a stand before signing any contract. I had no parents or lawyers to accompany me so other players always ended up with a better deal.

Casimiro Marin was a Brazilian player who played for Boa Vista, a team from Minas Gerais that went touring in Europe. After playing two or three games that they lost by high scores, the Brazilian federation decided that they should return to Brazil because they were obviously not qualified to play their scheduled games. Some of the players returned to Brazil while others decided to stay in Europe and try their luck. Marin stayed in Spain for some time then he went to Germany. From Germany, he heard about the Philadelphia Ukrainians. That was when I met him. I was young and inexperienced, so he taught me how to deal with the Ukrainians during my reassignments. While the Ukrainians brought new players every year, my salary remained the same. At that time, I needed money to pay for college. I argued with them, and then they decided to sell me to New York. During the week, many Ukes were not happy, so they negotiated me back for two thousand more dollars, which was good money at the time. This showed that they did care for me. I used this money to put myself through college and eat whenever I had enough money.

The cup game with United Scots from Los Angeles caused Marin to get fired. When he was told that he was not starting because they brought back Michael Noha from Argentina, Marin returned his game shirt to the coach immediately. I begged him not to do it because eventually he would get back in the game, and he was still earning money whether he played or not. Insane or not, he took his shirt off, and that was it. We couldn't believe that the Ukes brought Michael Noha back not knowing of his physical condition, and he started in that game instead of the guy who had saved us in Philadelphia. The game was a disaster, and we lost 3 to 1. We came back to Philadelphia, and Marin was unemployed, so I gave him part of my pay weekly so that he could eat. I tried to put him in contact with a New York team, but when he moved to New York, things did not work well for him. One evening, I received a call from him that he was taken by the police and landed in a crazy house in Long Island. He couldn't speak good English so that didn't help. From the University of Maryland, I came to Philadelphia looking for a friend to accompany me to New York and get Marin out of that hospital. The only friend whom I could find was Valdir Mendonca whom I had brought from Brazil the previous year. We drove to Long Island. By telling them that I was an assistant professor at the University of

Maryland, we managed to get him out of there and brought him back to Philadelphia. He wasn't totally "there," but I housed him and fed him and got him a ticket to go back to Brazil. In the meantime, he had sent for his younger brother to come to the US to visit him. So one day his brother called me from JFK Airport, saying that he didn't have any money to come to Philadelphia. I paid his trip by phone, and now I had two people to take care of. Casimiro never told me about his brother coming to America. That was a very unpleasant surprise and imposition. I tried to find them a job and get them out of my house because I couldn't support them any longer. Finally, Casimiro went back to Brazil, and his brother moved to South Philadelphia. Casimiro became a little unstable due to a lot of disappointments in his soccer career, but he was a true friend. His brother found a girl and got married. I ran into him a couple of years later, and he was doing okay. He had a job and seemed happy in South Philly. To Casimiro Marin Sanches, I owe a lot about the game; he taught me some special moves and very much about ball control, speed with and without the ball, and how to negotiate a contract, a matter in which I was very naive. We practiced together in the afternoons. He would sleep late every morning. Under his control, my game got much better at that time with the Philadelphia Ukrainians and with the other teams that I played for.

CHAPTER ELEVEN

In 1959, the Ukranians decided to sell the famous Mike Noha to Chicago Lyons. They knew that after five goals he scored against the Los Angeles Kickers, it was an epic event that would never come back, the Ukes had forgotten that there were other players involved in that fantastic game. The arrangement made between the two teams included a game in Chicago and the money made in that transaction would be solidified. To go from Philadelphia to Chicago by car or by bus, it would be too long of a ride, so the Philadelphia Ukrainians decided to rent a plane to take us to Chicago and to Detroit for another game. The players and the management were all excited to take that trip. We all went to the airport thinking we were traveling in a classy airplane. However, they had rented a smaller aircraft in which you could fit about thirty people. Obviously it wasn't a new aircraft when I saw it; it seemed like a dangerous craft. The players got kind of hysterical, but we all fitted in it, so I guess it was all right. The crew started the engines and the aircraft moved into the takeoff lane; I was afraid. As the pilots warmed up the engines, all the players were drinking and singing having a great time. Once we were airborne, the weather turned bad on us. There was lightning and thunder. We were flying scared because the airplane began to go up and down into the dark clouds; some drops were deep and truly scary. The airplane began to drop into no air and pick up its altitude again. I frankly thought the end was near. By that time, some players became quiet while others were still joking and playing around. After one hour of this flight, we finally arrived at Chicago O'Hare airport. I was very upset with that trip. We were very well received by the Chicago Ukrainians. We had a good game, which ended in a tie.

After the game, they presented us with a fantastic dinner. To make the atmosphere more pleasant, they presented us with a show where the Ukrainian girls played an instrument called "bandura." I personally enjoyed the dinner and the music offered in our honor. The Chicago Ukrainians really displayed great affection and respect toward us. After eating and drinking a few beers, we were no longer concerned about the metallic airplane waiting to take us to Detroit then to Philadelphia. There was a schedule we had to meet. We were leaving Chicago at 6:00 p.m. on Friday to play a game in Detroit on Sunday. We left the Ukrainian Club at around 5:00 p.m. Many players got lost and they came a little late. The airplane started its preparations, but for some ungodly reason, the engines wouldn't start. So all the passengers that were there got off the plane and were pushing the plane to get it started. In the meantime, some of the missing players came running down the runway trying to get on the plane, which had finally started. Some of us were at the plane's entrance helping them get in the plane. That flight wasn't too bad. Everything seemed to be working all right. We made it in time and won the game in Detroit.

On Sunday night, we prepared for the trip back to Philadelphia. Once again, we had to worry about getting the airplane started and put it on the runway for takeoff. Once in the air, the weather turned bad on us again. This time, most people weren't laughing; they were praying instead. The plane began to take some long falls in between the clouds, causing the people that weren't using their seat belts to hit the ceiling. Some of us had beer or soda in our hands that splashed all over us. This time, God had mercy on us because we arrived safely in Philadelphia. As far as I am concerned, no more trips like that one. It showed us how insignificant our lives are. A week later, after that trip, I read in the papers that that very same plane had crashed, killing all the army recruits that were on board. In my thoughts, we were extremely lucky and thankful for being alive to continue with our lives.

CHAPTER TWELVE

From the beginning of my era with the Ukes, we played a number of international games. We received a visit from Manchester City and Manchester United in 1959. They were a good team then and have continued their growth until today. We weren't that great, but we played an even game with them. I had no idea that Manchester United would someday reach the greatness of the present time. We tied them 3 to 3. Then Manchester City, which was also a great team, came; and it was also a tie. The English had great teams at that time, and they were world-famous. Many of their players played for the national team.

While all of this was going on, the Ukrainians were winning their league and also the cups. In 1962, I went to Brazil looking for players for the Ukrainian team. I went to the newspapers and put some ads out for players to come to my house for interviews. I wound up selecting three players, M. V. Dinho, Tim Viola, and Osvaldo Cunha. When they came to the US, they were successful because I had also brought a coach with them. The coach's name was Marcos Pawlowsky. He came from a team called Guarani from Paraguay's professional division. These players found it hard to believe that I also played soccer! They were extremely surprised when they saw me changing for the game at Lighthouse field. We won the game, and I played a good part in leading the team to that victory. It took some time for the Brazilians to get adjusted in the US until they started playing better.

M. V. Dinho was the first that I saw at a game in São Paulo. He was a strong and pushy goal-scoring forward. I didn't know anything about dope being used in soccer at that time. M. V. Dinho was involved in it. He needed to receive some dope from South America to perform well. He had scored six goals in three games, and when he wasn't able to get his product from Brazil, his performance started to decline. When the cold and snowy winter came, the Brazilians started having trouble in the game here and wanted to go back to warm Brazil. Tim Viola went back first because he just couldn't deal with the weather.

Mr. Pawlowsky was an intelligent coach. He knew how to put the team on the field, thus winning all the games, but the cold got to him also. Apparently, he was not prepared for it. For someone who is used to warm weather, the winter can be really shocking.

The Ukrainians had a very good team in the early sixties. We won all of our league games. There were occasions when we were called for the all-star games. The game that stands out in my mind was when five of our players were called to play against England's world cup team. This was right before England went to Brazil and beat their national team in Rio de Janeiro 1 to 0. They were world cup winners in 1962. I was somewhat experienced in playing a few foreign teams, but I never expected to play against England. I was shocked and surprised to be on the same field as Bobby Charlton and Jackie Charlton. That game was an example of legitimate soccer. The English players were all in extremely good shape. I only went in at the second half. My duty was to mark Jackie Charlton. I was young and strong and decided to give him a run for his money. The game was 8 to 0 when I went in, and the game ended at 9 to 1. I really went after Jackie and used all my weapons possible. I just couldn't handle him. He was the best player I ever played against. I tried to stop him any way possible, but I wasn't able to. At the end of the game, my legs were so sore that I could hardly even walk. We weren't prepared for such a game. This game added a lot to my experience. I had been more careful in collecting balls and in passing ahead of my opponents to prevent losing unnecessary balls. This game opened my eyes for other international games that came during the New York International League. I felt more confident and able, seldom losing the ball. I did have a big problem. I was goal-shy, even though I created a lot of plays and plays that resulted in goals. I had a hard time scoring myself. I can only remember a few goals that I scored and some that I missed.

In International League, I missed an impossible goal against Nice of France. After a give-and-go with Sanchez, I wound up in front of the net with the goalie completely beat. I tried to place it in the corner, but the ball hit the post and bounced out. I guess if Ricardo Montalban and Gina Lolobrigita were watching that game, they must have been disappointed at that play. God bless them both. One goal that I didn't miss was against Phoenix of the USL of Pennsylvania for the open cup. They played us very tough on a muddy field. I was fine playing on a muddy field. When you would fake an opposing player, they would fall in the mud while I was having fun. Phoenix gave us a very tough game. They had lots of good players such as Ed Enberger, Whitey, Diego Burbano, Ray Grossmullet, etc. They really had the Ukrainians cornered when toward the end of the game I picked the ball of the mud and put it in the air to the corner of the net that not even famous Whitey could catch. That shot decided the game. I can also remember a goal in Brazil from about forty yards out. I was playing for a club named Apis at an industrial championship in São Paulo on a Saturday afternoon. We were playing against an army team. We had a few players missing. There was a free kick outside of the penalty area that I was to take. The goalie said he needed no wall. That statement got me a little upset. It seemed that the goalie didn't believe in my shot. I set the ball up and took a long distance to hit it. I aimed the ball at the goalie. I hit the ball so hard, and as it traveled, it changed directions in the air. The goalie thought he had it, but it dropped, fooling him completely.

Another powerful shot that I took was when I was playing for the Metropolitano Soccer Club in São Paulo. We were playing against a team from Mooca called Portuguesinha. They had a very good team, and there was a free kick from forty yards again. The other team had a wall set up. I kicked it with all of my might and hit one of their players in the head, deflecting the ball in the net. He went down. Thank God, he was okay. I always worried about accidents during games. During my playing years, I had been threatened many times. Because of my background, I was prepared to face even the worst enemy, but with good intentions!

CHAPTER THIRTEEN

Education

When I first arrived in America during the summer of 1956, I was seventeen years old. In Brazil, I started doing better with my evening school. Of course, I had to work during the day. After a long day's work, I was already tired, but I went to night school every night to make up for the blunders I did while in day school. This was the turning point in my life. I started to get better grades and busied myself with schoolwork. My English teacher was very good. He made us learn the ABCs by singing with an accordion that he brought to class. I was cutting classes in my day school, and I would go to the movies downtown. They were mostly spoken in English. I listened to the vocabulary and phrases, and it helped me learn the English language better. I had the intention of going to school, but college was just not on my mind at the time.

When I played amateur soccer for VE, I went to night school also. That was what helped me complete the requirements for high school in the United States. When I was informed that I had made the US Olympic team, many colleges stared sending me letters. According to what I was told, there was a person taking entrance exams and you could get in with no problems. So I started thinking, *"What do I have to lose?"*

During the soccer season in Philadelphia, a "friend" borrowed one hundred dollars from me for no serious reason. I didn't know how to handle money then, and I lent it to him. So when winter came and times got hard, I began to go after my money. When I pressured him, he told me that I was a fool for not using his indicated person to take my entrance exam to Temple University. I was not aware that this fact could hurt me more than help me. That person, who at that point was no longer a friend, was not going to pay me back, thus forcing me to enter this dishonest deal with him. I had no idea of the problems that this could cause me. His friend scored extremely high in the exam, and this drew the attention of the people checking the results. Consequently, I got called in New Jersey and passed by very unpleasant moments. I was humiliated and really trashed out. When I went home, I was very depressed because I allowed myself to get involved in that messy situation.

A few months after that unpleasant event took place, I received news from the University of Maryland, which accepted me because I was in the upper half, grade-wise, in my graduating class. In the meantime, I had visited the campus of Michigan State and was very impressed. They also had offered me a full ride. I had a friend there, Rubens Filizola, who attended Michigan State, and he wanted to see me there playing by his side. Because I was a player for the Ukranians in Philadelphia, I was inclined to go to Maryland through my own merits. This proved that the people who wanted me involved in dishonest means to get into the college were wrong. I should have waited for my honest opportunity.

While the coach of Maryland, Mr. Royal P. Doyle, helped me overcome this horrible entrance procedure, there were other coaches moved by jealousy who were fighting to discredit me. One of them was the coach of West Chester, who accused me of being a professional ballplayer. In those days, I played for the Ukrainians under amateur form. We got our expenses paid, and that was all. This coach managed to rule me ineligible to play for the University of Maryland. As soon as the news broke out, I figured I was out on the street. Mr. Royal, whom I have the highest consideration for, allowed me to continue in the campus and help him coach the team as an assistant.

I had several problems with the athletes living in our dormitory. One of the lacrosse players packed my things and put everything in front of the building in the snow. I was alone in America, and I didn't know what to do. I went back in and told that player that I was going out for a cup of coffee and would be back in one hour. If my things were not put back in their proper place, I would wait until he fell asleep and would give him what he deserved. He was over six feet tall and very strong. I really don't know what happened, but he put all of my belongings back in their place. Apparently, he got scared, knowing that because of my situation I would probably hurt him.

At that time, I had lost my scholarship and I had no means of support except what I got from soccer whenever we played. I had a decent meal every day with the soccer team, but Mr. Royal could no longer justify giving it to me. I would have to find a way to eat. I used a fake ID, and when they got wise to me or I had nobody at the front whom I knew, I began to sneak in through the back door. Those doors were very tricky; they were made to prevent what I was trying to do. I studied them and got to them before they locked by stopping them with my foot. Since I was very thin, I made it in with no big problems.

I loved college life. It was what I needed to refresh myself after the Philadelphia Ukrainian games. My weekend routine was to leave Maryland after classes on Friday around three in the afternoon, and I would arrive in Philadelphia around six or seven in the evening. I went directly to practice and after that to the club and stayed until eleven in the evening or later. On Saturdays, we would rest for the game on Sunday. All of this was contingent on winning. If we lost the game, it was not wise to go to the club because they would not pay you until Wednesday after their other weekly practice. The other problem was to face the public. They weren't used to losing and were not very receptive after losses.

Every once in a while, we would lose a game, and that would make our fans mad even against specific players. They would get booed on the field and then persecuted after the game by some of the more fanatical members. The Ukes were a national team; the people were mainly interested in winning. There were no excuses for losing;

we represented their country. The team was well-known in Europe, and according to what they told me, they were in the Russian encyclopedia. I believed them; I never heard anyone saying that it was not true. The Ukrainians had great support from their people, and they also had many pretty young ladies attending our games. Some of the players married them. I was one of them. My children have Ukrainian blood in them. I have four children out of that marriage.

The University of Maryland became my second home. I loved being there, trying to pursue an education. I loved the campus, the stadium, especially their basketball court, Cole Field House, which was then the largest in the south of the USA. I enjoyed the cafeteria where I met many new friends. It was an escape from the soccer world. I wasn't a great student, but I attended every class that I had and tried to stay awake in some of the boring ones. My English was very poor so I had to retake some of the English courses even when barely passing. I decided to specialize in foreign languages, mainly in Spanish and German. I was good in Spanish because I had to use the language on Sundays when playing with the Argentinians. German was a lot harder for me because I didn't use it as much as my original language Portuguese. The university used me to help establish Portuguese as a new course while I was a graduate assistant. That really helped me build a love for teaching.

Being an assistant language teacher at Maryland helped me when I went to Brazil to look for players. In Brazil, they put me on the front page of the newspapers. That took place in the early 1960s in São Paulo, one of the largest cities in the world.

While I was in college, I saw the funeral of President Kennedy while I was wandering around downtown Washington, District of Columbia. On my trips from Maryland to Philadelphia, I would drive an old Ford V8 '56 that had eight cylinders or an old Plymouth that saved me money in gasoline. When I didn't have a car, I took the bus that left me in Baltimore, and from there, I took a local bus that left me at the entrance of the university.

On my second year as a graduate assistant, I lost my brother in Brazil. It was my brother's day off in the army, but the troops were called in because there was a rebellion warning in São Paulo. He was helping them as a mechanic for war trucks and any motorized equipment. He had learned a lot from my father. That particular day, there were a bunch of bees buzzing around their quarters and the soldiers were complaining about them. He was the only repairman who was available to take care of the problem. Because we had eucalyptus trees at our house, he got himself a bag and a knife and climbed up that huge eucalyptus tree. When he got up there, the bees attacked him; he lost his balance and fell. These trees are very high off the ground, so when he fell, that impact crushed his skull. By the time he got to the hospital, it was too late. As a result, I lost my job as a graduate assistant because it was during the college season. It was another opportunity lost of pursuing a higher position at the University of Maryland. Once again under devastating circumstances.

In 1956, I got married. She was a Ukrainian girl and the most beautiful I had ever met. I went back to Brazil and started my teaching career there. In order for anyone to teach in Brazil legally, you would need a teaching certificate that comes from Brasilia, which is the capital city of Brazil. I needed to take several courses in Brazil to complement my University of Maryland diploma. While I was teaching at Colegio São Judas Tadeu in Mooca, I was taking evening courses in Mogy das Cruzes University. In order for me to do this, I had to catch a train three nights a week for about an hour ride back and forth. Since I didn't have many friends, I was alone most of the time during those trips.

I had to take these courses to fulfill the necessary requirements to obtain official permission to teach from Brasilia. One of the courses was psychology. The teacher was an elderly lady who also taught in other colleges in São Paulo. The first exam she gave to the class of about forty students while I was sitting in the back on the right side alone as usual. The students in front of the room were constantly volunteering answers during her classes. The next class conducted after the exam was two days later. She came into the classroom, smiling and happily telling the class that one of the students in her class had the highest score in all of the three colleges that she taught.

Then she started giving back the papers. She gave about ten papers back when she came upon the highest scoring exam. She immediately called on a student who was in front of her who was always participating. She went to him and said, "Alexandre Ely, please stand up so the class can see you." He was embarrassed and told her, "My name is not Alexandre Ely." She was surprised and said, "Well, who is Alexandre Ely?" I was sitting in the corner of the last row. I stood up. "I am Alex Ely, ma'am." All the students were surprised. After this episode, I all of a sudden had many friends, even during the train trips. In Brazil, I was teaching English as a second language at all levels. I even had my own course at the Colegio São Judas supervised by my boss, Dr. Alberto Mesquita, who had a great future in building that facility.

After I obtained the courses I needed, it then took two more years to obtain the document that enabled me to teach English in Brazil. While teaching English, I learned a lot about grammar and became very professional in that field. The textbooks that we had to use were very bad. I finally decided one day to write a textbook. It was to present the subject in a more user-friendly way and to keep the students' interest alive. During one of my vacations, I started the preparation for my book. I had my wife typing the material, and I also had the help of my dear friend, Mr. Antonio Fonseca.

The summer of 1967 was totally taken up by my book. I couldn't find any publishers interested in my work. So I published the book with the father of one of my students who owned a publishing shop. The first edition came out very poor. Many pictures were in the wrong places. Even so, I managed to sell one thousand copies. I was very happy with the sales. It came time to make the financial settlement with the owner of the printing shop, and he refused to pay me. I got tired of it and told him that if he ran any more copies of the book, I would sue him. I was greatly disappointed to say the least, but I did not give up.

I went to a bookstore downtown called *Discubra*. They showed interest, so we ordered two thousand books that they somehow sold. He said he needed another three thousand copies. So we convinced the printer to do them. When this whole deal was finished, I didn't get paid, so I was completely distraught with these book dealers.

They were very smart and hard to catch. Now I had the book and forbade its sales to *Discubra*.

I went back into teaching, and I found one student whose father was an editor of a company called *Editora Nacional*. I personally gave him my book and expected them to accept it. After several weeks, I got very mad because I hadn't heard from them so I called them back. He told me to come by the publishing company. He then explained to me that they had three English books that were doing very well, so there was no room for my book. I took my book and angrily walked out of there.

As I walked back into São Paulo city, I was on Ipiranga Avenue when I decided to have a drink to calm me down. I entered a bar and ordered a double shot. I drank it really quick and went back to the street. I was near São Joao Avenue when I heard someone calling me. It was a friend of mine who sold books in *Colégio São Judas Tadeu*. I was not in a talking mood, but I told him what had just happened. He told me not to worry, that there was a new publishing house in town. They didn't have an English book. My friend and I walked all the way across town trying to get to the publishing house before it closed at six in the evening. We got to the building when they were closing their doors. We didn't know that the owner, Dr. Anderson Dias Fernandes, was still in there. He met us and invited us to his office. He looked over the book and told us he would let us know in a week. We left the area happy knowing that at least we got the book to be looked at. He had taken my phone number to get in touch with me and to let me know the outcome in a week. We came there on a late Friday evening. Waiting for a week wasn't too bad. I completed the night hanging around the nightclubs in an area called Liberdade.

On Monday morning, I received the call. They decided to publish my textbook whose title then was *A New Approach to English*. I had no idea what that meant for me. I figured they were going to publish about two thousand books. Instead, they shocked me by publishing one hundred thousand books and in the same year had five new editions. One day, I went to the office and asked for an advance in money. They gave me a check with so many zeroes. I had never seen anything like it. After this, many colleges became interested in me. The publishers came after me for a second book. Since I had broken the initial half of the first volume presented, I presented the second book, which was mostly prepared ahead of time. This gave a sequence to the initial work. This time, Dr. Anderson got a team of teachers to evaluate my work, and they did not approve of it. I was again disappointed, but I pleaded with Dr. Anderson that I was right and the board of teachers was wrong. He finally decided to give it a try. They had thirty thousand books printed, and they were all sold quickly.

In the same year, he had three large editions published approaching almost a million books. At that time, I progressed quickly financially. With that income, I bought a house in an upper-class neighborhood in São Paulo. I also bought twenty-four thousand square meters of land in an area called Marsilac near São Paulo.

The textbooks motivated me to write a novel that I called *A Destiny at Dawn*. I paid to get it published. I believe the novel will eventually sell because it is now being offered in major bookstores and through the Internet in the USA.

After the book had been out for three years, the colleges and universities in Brazil started pressing me for my master's degree. I thought of coming back to the US and entering a program in some college in the Philadelphia area. Since I was familiar with Temple, I went there. Upon examining my undergraduate grades, I was told they were too low to enter graduate school. I had brought my two textbooks around to show them my history. The department head of Temple's graduate school decided to give me a chance by giving me three courses, and I accepted eagerly. My future depended on how I did with these three courses. Consequently, I got admitted into Temple's graduate program.

In the meantime, I got a teaching position at Cardinal Dougherty High School. While I was teaching regular school hours, I tried to schedule my graduate classes in the afternoons, evening, and weekends, and heavily in the summer. Temple's graduate ESOL program got me exhausted. Some of the courses were borderline ridiculous. I took a movie course where we watched old movies and wrote reports on them. Since I had been teaching English in Brazil, many of the courses were reasonable to my understanding. I never realized it, but at the end, my grades were the highest in the whole program. My supervisor told me that I didn't have to take the final comprehensive exams. She then suggested that I take it anyway because it was good for me. I was just glad to graduate and move on with my life. From that day forward, I promised myself never to take any graduate courses again; I was severely weathered out.

CHAPTER FOURTEEN

Pelé and I

Pelé and I are almost the same age. Pelé was already a known player when I started playing in the USA. I always admired the great Pelé, not only for his ability as a player but also for being humble and friendly to people. I watched him grow into soccer since the first World Cup when he was only sixteen. I lived in São Paulo and followed the games daily. When he first appeared in the national team, he was my idol. I never thought that someday I would meet him personally.

In 1965, coming back from an elimination game in Mexico, I was already secretly married. I was then very recognized for my efforts in these elimination games. The United States federation elected me as the best player of the USA in those games. I was very disappointed with that Walt Chyzowycz episode during the Mexico World Cup elimination game. When I came back to Philadelphia, I had to face another tough player and Coach Juan Borodiak. Soon after I arrived, he started using me up front with the Ukrainian team. Then we had our last season game in New York. There I was again being elected as the best player in the US. I felt very honored, but I knew in the back of my head that I would be leaving. I never told anybody that I was going back to Brazil. I just left.

Once I was in my birth country, I was twenty-five and still in great shape. I went to try out for São Paulo FC where I met Francisco Sarno, a former professional player. He introduced me to the coach Mr. Aimore Moreira. I started working out with São Paulo FC. Sarno found out who I was, and we became friends. He was writing a book called *Futebol: A Danca do Diabo*. Since he had no background in education, he asked me to review the book for him. The English translation for the title was *Soccer: Devil's Dance*. Sarno expressed many of the good and bad things that happened to him during his soccer career. He played in Fluminense, Palmeiras, Santos, and Vasco da Gama and was a well-known player. Sarno liked me, but he told me that he didn't believe that people with a long career in the school field should play soccer.

It was through Sarno that I went to Santos and started working out with their team. I met most of the players right away because Professor Mazzei stopped the practice and introduced me to all of the players. Only Pelé wasn't there that day. I got a chance to personally get to know many famous Brazilian World Cup soccer players. Since I had no car, Professor Mazzei, Gilmar, and some other player picked me up because I lived on the way to Santos. For me, it was a great experience. They gave me a locker, and I placed my soccer equipment in there. After practice, there was a hot bath pool that was used to relax at the end of the tough workouts on the field. I did it most of the time because in the ISA I had never seen anything like that. I became close friends with Pepe and Professor Mazzei. Every practice, Pepe and I stayed late to shoot at the goalies. I was a good shooter, but Pepe was very powerful. Other than these guys, I also met Zito, Formiga, Laercio, Ramos Delgado, Lima, Turcao, Mengalvio, Gilmar, Pelé, Pepe, Rildo, Clodoaldo, Coutinho, and some other juniors who later became famous.

During that time, Queen Elizabeth came to visit Brazil. Pelé was introduced to her. At the same time, New York Cosmos became interested in Pelé and a few other Santos players. Since I was there anyway, they asked me to teach English to the interested players. I was doing the two things I loved most—to teach and to play soccer. There were articles in the São Paulo newspapers about me. In the meantime, I felt the pressure of earning more money to keep my family because times were hard.

From that time that I had met Pelé, we couldn't expand our friendship due to his constant traveling and taking care of his business. Professor Mazzei was close to me at the time. The coach of Santos was Antoninho, also a great person. Due to family needs, I wasn't able to continue making those daily trips and the chances of having a contract weren't that good. I began to look for a teaching job in São Paulo. When I finally got a teaching job at Brasilux, a commercial college, other jobs began to appear. Since I made more money teaching, I played soccer on the weekends for Metropolitano SC, on Saturday for Tabatinguera FC in downtown São Paulo and Apis an industrial team in Vila Mariana, São Paulo. I spent six years teaching and playing soccer on weekends in Brazil.

I decided to go back to the United States to get my master's degree, and that was when my life got involved again with Pelé and Professor Mazzei. I was invited to coach at the Pelé Soccer Camps, and there I saw Pelé and his son Edinho. By that time, I had my two boys, Alex Jr. and Edward, who met Pelé's son and became friends. Pelé would come and give his soccer demonstrations for the kids on Fridays. His ability in showing the kids how to do bicycle kicks was incredible. They learned many maneuvers and ball control and were also able to witness Pelé's great shooting. My kids learned plenty from Pelé's demonstrations with Professor Mazzei explaining to the kids in English. Sometimes the professor wasn't immediately available, and then Pelé would ask me to be his interpreter. I enjoyed those moments; after all, he was the best in the world of soccer.

I had the opportunity of being in Pelé's company at the coaches' party. I told him a lot of jokes that he seemed to enjoy. We laughed and he played his songs. If you didn't know, Pelé is a great samba player, singer, and composer. During the camp, we had a heavy schedule to follow. We had prebreakfast exercises. We had a meeting prior to the beginning of each camp day. All coaches were assigned their daily tasks, and they should have always stuck to Professor Mazzei's agenda.

Inside of a week, the children were really learning some of Pelé's abilities. I was pleasantly surprised when Pelé would come to lunch and sit by me. We had many interesting conversations about soccer, life, and other things that were on his mind at the time. I've learned to appreciate Pelé more as a person because he was generally a positive voice in the lives of many people.

One day, I saw Pelé's son in the woods of the college campus. I went to him and told him that it was dangerous to let his son that far from him in the woods. Pelé sent someone to get his son right away. At night, most of us would go out to eat or have a few drinks. Pelé never came along, but his brother Zoca enjoyed those evenings with us.

I was teaching a Portuguese class in Philadelphia for the public school system for a good number of years on Saturday mornings. We had mostly adults and some younger kids. We used to take trips in the spring mostly to New York. We would have a great Brazilian meal and would find some places of cultural interest to visit. Pelé was playing for the New York Cosmos at that time. I told my students that we were going to meet Pelé. They thought I was joking. So we planned on one Saturday in the spring to go to New York, have a Brazilian meal, and watch the soccer game in Randal's Island. We took two cars that were loaded with students that were all dying to meet the great Pelé, not really knowing if they were going to get the opportunity.

First, we went to eat around Forty-fourth Street in New York. After everyone ate, we went to the stadium. We found comfortable seats and watched a very good game. After the game, we went down to the outside of the player's locker room. I looked through the door and saw Pelé being interviewed by some television channel under some intense lights. I told my students to wait outside. I approached Pelé's bodyguard, Pedro, and gave him my card, telling him that I brought my class from Philadelphia to meet Pelé. After Pedro gave him my card, Pelé left the people who were interviewing him and came outside smiling, gave me a hug, and shook the hands of all of my students, thanking them for coming. The students were all shocked. I myself was extremely surprised at how gracious he was. That was the greatest gift that I received from Pelé.

On our way back to Philadelphia, there was hardly any talking amongst the students. They were all really surprised that they were able to shake hands with the great Pelé. These are the kind of events that really only occur once in a lifetime.

After that fantastic event, I was taking a trip to Brazil by Varig Airlines, not knowing that the great Pelé was on the same flight. My son, Alex Jr., was along with me; and we met yet again. He told me that he wasn't sure if his brother was going to come to Congonhas airport to pick him up. I said to Pelé that many people would be glad to give him a ride to Santos. I told him that he should have people who would take him with no problems. Pelé replied that the real friends that he had, he could count on his fingers. That gave me something to think about. *How true his philosophy was*, I thought at the time.

The German Old Timers soccer team appeared at Pelé's camp for a visit. Since most of the coaches working there were former players, they decided to play an exhibition game against them. I enjoyed the chance of playing with all of those coaches. Germany had among their players Uwe Seeler, Libuda, and many other former World Cup stars. We brought that whole soccer camp to see this game. Pelé was our goaltender and his brother, Zoca, played in the middle field; and I got stuck with left fullback. Every time Pelé received the ball, he would throw it to me; and I would start building from the left side. I put in a few good crosses, and the game ended in a tie. I told Pelé to take it easy because I wasn't in shape, but he just kept on sending me the ball. After the game, Uwe Zeller came to talk to me and said he knew me from somewhere. I said all right, but I had never met him until that very day.

Just a comparison between Pelé and Beckenbauer. We met many times, and the kids would come after Pelé to sign autographs, and Pelé would stay there doing so much that Professor Mazzei would end up having to drag him away. As for Bekenbauer, kids came after him and Bekenbauer told them to see him during the meetings or would take their addresses and mail it to them. That is the difference among those stars of yesterday. They prefer to spend their time with the people who made them big. To me, Pelé is the greatest soccer player that ever played the game. He unites his soccer ability with his charismatic humbleness and desire to do well for himself and others.

CHAPTER FIFTEEN

There are many great soccer players in the world, and I have been very fortunate to meet some of them personally or in some soccer circumstance. I have described my friendship with Pelé, and I've also met Rivelino, Uwe, Zeller, Beckenbauer, Orlando, Gilmar, and many others.

In 1963, I was invited to play for Toronto City in the Canadian Championship. Toronto had signed up the great Hungarian player, Ladislao Kubala. They needed some player that could play with Kubala in more or less his style. Somehow, my name came up, and they decided to give me a call in Philadelphia. They explained that they needed someone who could join forces with Kubala and make Toronto City a winning team. I had some idea who Kubala was because I had read his name in some soccer magazines. He came to Toronto, and I had moved to Toronto to play for their soccer club. I was on vacation from school in Philadelphia. I wasn't in shape because the Ukrainians finished their season a month before. So I was having a good time dating some girls and enjoying that summer when this opportunity appeared.

In Montreal, Canada, I had a girlfriend who was Ukrainian-French-Canadian. She found out where I was living and came to see me. She came on Saturday morning, and I was very happy to see her because I was in love with her. What really stopped us from getting married at that time was the distance from Philadelphia to Montreal.

During that same year, we had a New Year's Eve date in Montreal but that weekend snowed so hard that the airports were closed and many of the highways toward Montreal were blocked. Since I couldn't show up, she possibly met someone else, and I thought I had lost her forever. The night before I would have to play along with Kubala, I spent with that girl. Since it was the first night ever, I overdid it, so in the morning, I woke up in no shape to play that important game on that Sunday. Regardless of my shape, due to my commitment, I had to go and play anyway. There was no chance of having me on the bench! I decided to shape up the best way that I could and do the best that I could on the field.

I had never met Kubala, and there I was to help him in the middle field. I always played with heart, and that day would be no different. We played like we were playing together for years. I exchanged passes with Kubala, and through these passes, he scored two goals. The game ended in a tie thanks to that great player. Kubala was more or less my height, but his body was tremendously strong. His shots on goal were powerful, always keeping the goaltender busy. Whenever I got the ball, he was easy to find so I would pass it to him. He was forty-two years old at that time.

After that game, I didn't feel too good and was ready to pass out when Kubala looked at me and said, "I know what is wrong with him, and I am going to take him to a special place to eat something." They took me to a Hungarian restaurant in Toronto. I had no idea where I was, but I just went along with Kubala and his friends. As soon as we sat down, Kubala ordered Hungarian goulash with potatoes. After eating this, I soon began to feel better. He spoke to me in Spanish; I understood him very well.

During that dinner, we were talking about the game and how well we played together. To my utmost surprise, Kubala invited me to go to Spain with him after the season ended. I did not know him that well and was not sure about my possibilities. I explained to him that I was in college and trying to obtain my bachelor of arts diploma. I wasn't ready to make that kind of a move. Not thinking or knowing who Ladislao Kubala really was, I really let that opportunity slide right through my fingers. Later, I came across his name in the Brazilian newspaper as being nominated the national coach of Spain for the upcoming World Cup. I was pleasantly surprised and sort of sorry for not going with him to Spain. At that time, I was in my early twenties and ready for a break like that. Because decisions of that nature had to be made on the spot, I wasn't ready to make them.

CHAPTER SIXTEEN

I don't know how different each individual player is on the field or off the field. I imagine that each individual player shows his abilities and character during the games they play. How they acquire these abilities and qualities comes from their background. Coaches are supposed to help players perform better.

In Brazil, many former players became coaches regardless of their schooling. Since the invention of the coaching schools here in the US, we have fewer professional coaches around. I was a student of some of the US coaching schools. I retain an A and B license to coach soccer in the US. Do you know how many jobs I've gotten from having these licenses? The answer is none. I define coaches as academic and veteran players. The question is, "Who knows best?"

Since I was a professional player and a former Olympic, Pan American, and World Cup player I started going to a Delaware campus for my B license. At that, time I was playing with the Ukrainians, and they offered to pay for several players to attend the coaching school. The head coach of that camp was Walt Chyzowycz being helped by Lenny Lucenko. As soon as Mike Noha found out who was running the camp, he turned his car around and left even though the Ukrainians had paid for his schooling. I was somewhat surprised, but I decided to stay and see what I could learn.

I worked with the outdoor and indoor classes run by people who knew a lot less about soccer than I did. I went through all the details, including trying very hard to stay out of trouble. My room-mate stayed in every night and studied heavily. When the final exam came, each coach selected a topic to talk about. I took the *catenaccio*, which relates to an Italian system brought about because of an air-plane crash that destroyed the Italian Torino team in the late 1950s. They decided to promote a defensive system to replace the players that died in that accident. I actually enjoyed what was going on at that camp.

One day I met Lenny Lucenko, and I was very naive in thinking of him as a friend; but I was about to learn a good lesson. Since I did not know how Lucenko had advanced in his school pursuits, I was told by him, "My name is Doctor Lucenko." Consequently, I excused myself and left the area. I kind of understood his motives, but I never spoke to him again. From my recollection, Lucenko used to travel with the Ukrainian nationals on trips to New York and Boston. He would entertain the players and passengers on the bus by singing Elvis Presley tunes. He was quite good at it. He went to college and became a doctor.

My impression of Walt and Lenny is that they were involved in an extremely difficult job of teaching coaches to evolve in this country. It amazes me that Walt developed a group of coaches who advanced in America getting the prestigious college coaching positions and, in my opinion, somehow making sure that there was nobody there to challenge them. They also got involved in the professional teams and in our federation. Some did well and some did not. The point I am trying to make is that soccer as a whole did not progress much during those years and many other talented coaches were left out.

My B license did not help me at the time so the next step was for me to get an A license, which was paid for by the United Soccer League of Pennsylvania. That took place at West Chester State University. When I appeared in the camp, nobody knew me. Little by little, I started to find people whom I knew. There were former play-ers and coaches from colleges all around the country. At that time, I was the all-star coach for the United Soccer League of Pennsylvania, and the league was doing well. This time the head coach wasn't Walt or Lenny; in fact, I can't remember who he was. I do remember that

Lew Mehel, George O'Neill, and Bohdan Sirick were present. At the beginning, they wanted all the students to run a mile. I pulled a muscle and could no longer participate in the physicals and was constantly with a trainer. After two days, I was feeling better and started kicking a ball around. Then there was the game between the coaches at the camp. The opposing team had all the good ballplayers. The only player I knew on my team was Bohdan Sirick. I played in the middle field and Bohdan played up front. At the end of the game, we had won with a score of 3 to 2. That is the best memory I have from these coaching camps.

Some of the coaches never had playing experience to be able to teach anything to the candidates. If they were teachers, then I could also be a teacher because I knew more than most of the instructors available. I agree that America needs a coaching school, but the Federation should bring in competent instructors instead of these instant homemade coaches. I feel that by accommodating certain people, the Federation is wasting its time and prolonging this never-ending pain of waiting for soccer to have success in the United States.

CHAPTER SEVENTEEN

After seven years away from the US, I had assumed a load of responsibilities. I had become a rather well-known educator in Brazil. My book, *A New Approach to English*, had sold an astronomical amount of copies all over the country. I felt the need to obtain my MA to advance my position as an educator. I decided to come back to the USA with these objectives in mind.

I already had two children to raise, and my wife wanted to see her family who never appreciated the fact that she married me. While I got accepted to the MA program at Temple University, I continued with my soccer activities. The Ukrainians were playing professionally in 1972. I attended their practices and played against their professional players.

One Friday night, I was practicing with them when one of their players kicked the ball with unusual force. I did what I normally do, step out to block the shot; but this young man kicked too hard, and it must have cracked the bone on top of the middle of his foot. I could swear it was not intentional, but it definitely forced this young man to go to the hospital and have his foot casted. When this incident happened, the team was being coached by Walter Tarnawski, a famous goalie from Argentina. Mike Yurchak, manager of the team, went to the club and told them to get rid of me because it was my fault of what happened to that young player. So they had a meeting in the club and then invited me in. From that negative event, they invited me to coach the team and to play whenever necessary. I didn't like the idea of playing, but I calculated and decided only if it was necessary. They politically counted on me to play the Ukrainian players who were signed, and among them was my brother-in-law, Nick Kuzewycz, who was a good player; and for that level, he did well. I played him most of the time whenever possible.

Sometimes the games got tough and some of the players changed their playing techniques. The Ukes signed five black players from Washington, but they were always late, which caused problems for the team. We were allowed two substitutes per half, and once you got out, you could not go in again. Sometimes I couldn't use them all in the same game, which did not bode well for them. At that time, we had some players from the Atoms who were decent. We took two goalies and Charlie Duccili. I had also brought Paul Nasser from Brazil. We had the potential of having a good team, and I trained them the best way that I could. I created the habit of sitting the players on Tuesday night to discuss our problems during the games. Sometimes some of the players got mad and wanted to further our discussions. I told them that these discussions were to help eliminate some of the obvious problems. Some players recognized the benefits, and others came to resent me.

I went to practices earlier to select the players whom I felt needed the extra work. The American players were my best crew. I took Ed Blaney, who played middle defender and showed him different tricks for heading the balls. Charlie Duccili was our goal man. I trained him for several weeks until he finally started to coordinate good shots. Charlie scored many important goals for us. Then we had Eddy Lee who loved to dribble. I tried to limit his dribbling making him more objective. Larry Sullivan was a strong fullback. I taught him to keep his position and only advance when there was no one to mark; he got really good in that position.

We had a game against New York Greeks. They even flew players in from Greece for that game. We were a group of local boys that went to New York and beat them 1 to 0 by a goal from Charlie. The Greek's coach approached me after the game and asked from what country I got my players. I had to explain that they were all American boys, but he just couldn't believe it.

I enjoyed coaching. However, along with making friends, you also make enemies. Some of the players have different points of view. Some were natural rebels, and there were others that had some unusual psychological profiles. They were also accompanied by some people in management who were almost totally deranged. The American players were the best to deal with. The Africans, South Americans, and Central Americans were more difficult to deal with.

When I first took the job as coach, I recruited Paul Nasser. He was a friend, and we also played together in Brazil for a club called Tabatinguera in downtown São Paulo. In Brazil, I would invite him to my farm on the weekends. He was an excellent player, and we really needed him. I did all of his paperwork for him to come to America. I went to Harrisburg to get him a player's Visa pass when the Ukes no longer wanted him. I never expected that a person that I worked so hard for to bring to this country would become my enemy in such a short amount of time. Slowly, our friendship disappeared as we did not see eye to eye in my coaching and in my playing choices.

I also had people who did not want me out of there and some who wanted me fired as coach. One day, I told Paul that if I got fired, the team would no longer exist. That is what happened as soon as I got fired. There was no more professional team in Philadelphia for the Ukrainian Nationals. I had other problems with that team with players whom I knew very little about their backgrounds. I had a player from Hungary, Andy Uhrin, who was a natural outside left. He was a good dribbler and had an excellent left foot shot. He was playing great as an outside left, but he insisted on playing middle field. I put him there, and his play wasn't as good. He kept insisting on this insanity until finally he had problems playing both positions. It is hard to please everyone when you are in a coaching position. Sometimes it is even hard to please one person. The Ukrainians quit the professional league and started building strong amateur teams. Most of their players lived in the Philadelphia area and played amateur ball in the new leagues that were starting.

CHAPTER EIGHTEEN

After being sidetracked in my schoolwork, my main goal again had become to obtain an MA at college in the United States. I wasn't interested in getting involved in soccer again. In the early seventies, the Atoms got started in Philadelphia, and their head coach was the famous Al Miller, who I had never met through the ranks of the US coaching schools. I wasn't playing professionally for a few years, so I was out of shape. I went to the Atoms to see what was going on. Al Miller gave me a linesman shirt and told me to be a linesman. I felt embarrassed but curiosity made me stay.

There were many players trying out, and amongst them was an Argentinian player who was really doing well. He was traveling from Mexico back to Argentina, stopping in Philadelphia for that tryout. Since I wasn't even able to step onto the field with the all-stars, I was called as an interpreter for the Argentinian. After practice, he called the players who interested him up to his office. I went with the Argentinian, and we waited for a while, and then they called me in and not the player to propose one thousand dollars a month. When I came back and told the Argentinian the amount of his offer, he told me to tell Al Miller to go f— himself. I told him that I couldn't go in there and say such a thing. He insisted, and I agreed only if he went in there with me. So we did.

Al Miller was sitting there all pleased with himself, but when I told him his answer, he got upset and threw us both out of his office.

I felt bad and tried to tell him that I was only the interpreter, but he wasn't hearing it. That is the way it went, and from that point on, I didn't feel as though I should go to any of the Atoms games. I felt like I was unwelcome there. What helped me overcome these disappointments was my family.

Now I find myself in the National Hall of Fame even with all of my disappointments throughout my soccer career. There were other incidents that pushed me close to the edge. I ran into J. D. Jorge, a player that I had helped when he came from Argentina. One day, I received a phone call from J. D., asking me to go shopping with him downtown. Since I was on a vacation, I said yes. As we wandered around the stores, we stopped at Wanamaker's by City Hall in Philadelphia. He was looking for a jacket, and there were many beautiful leather jackets around. He tried several jackets on until he found one that fit him. He put the jacket on and walked out of the building. I was scared. I said, "You don't do this here! You can get arrested for it!" He laughed and continued walking down Market Street like nothing happened. Next place he saw was a bookstore. He said he needed a dictionary. Somehow he walked out of there with a good-sized dictionary. This time we walked fast away from that bookstore. That was the last time I went shopping with J. D.! The Ukrainians were very happy with J. D. because he gave them some items to be used outside of their club.

J. D. was very upset with me for playing for the USA. That must have been his biggest dream, and he blamed me for not talking to the US coaches for him. As far as I knew, he wasn't even a citizen, and it was not my job to recruit players for the US team. Somehow we became enemies. I can remember his shouts on the soccer field, "EEEEELY!" like I was always guilty of some sort of infraction. His own teammates from Argentina disliked him immensely for the same reasons.

The tricks that some of the other players played were when we traveled to New York or Massachusetts. We would stop at a diner and the whole team would eat and of course each player would receive a certain amount of dollars to feed themselves. Unknown to the management team, one player would collect our tickets and money and say that he would pay and we could all go back into the bus. Guess what? That money was never paid. That player would go into the bathroom for a little while then back onto the bus with the money and the checks that were never paid because they were flushed down the toilet. I never thought of it until I saw some of the guys laughing, one of them told me what really happened. One game that we played in New Jersey and one of the players stole a whole set of forks and knives. It seemed to me that they did it for fun. I thought I was smart, but I lost big time to those fellows.

I can't say that I was a saint, but there are certain things that I would never do, especially to hurt friends, family, or other teammates. Some of those people were very cruel, selfish, and never cared in any way about anybody.

CHAPTER NINETEEN

From 1965 to 1972, while I was in Brazil, soccer seemed to have grown new leagues and players came from all over the world to the US. I had been in Brazil, trying to further my education. After returning to the US, I heard good and bad things about what happened to the game that I love. One of the Ukrainian players burned a Ukrainian flag before a soccer game. That is one thing that even I would not tolerate. Lots of new faces began to appear all over the place, and the professional league was going on with the Atoms in Philadelphia.

The management of the Atoms brought some lower-division English players and as usual tried to build a team around them. Again the local players got the shaft. I went down to see what was going on, hoping that some of the boys I knew would get picked. One name in particular broke my heart. It was Ed Blaney. Al Miller did not see anything in that boy who was my best player for the Ukrainians. His selections were borderline ridiculous. Even today, if the local talent is ignored, I will not attend any of the games.

For soccer to grow in the United States, we need to promote the American players and not make foreign players American just so they can play for the US. It is nice to see some of the clubs hiring Alexi Lalas and Jeff Agus as presidents. I just wonder how much input they have in that environment now that they are both in the National Hall of Fame. American players need good coaches. The reality is that many coaches are going overseas because there is just not much going on here.

My grandson, David Mesquita, just went to Brazil seeking help in order to advance in soccer. Here in America, we are sending our players out of the country to seek improvement. All of the famous older players are not working in their area to help the young players. This is due to the direction that our leaders were taking us.

After the Ukrainians closed their professional team, they placed their amateur team in the Third Division of the USL of Pennsylvania. I started teaching languages in the Catholic School system in Philadelphia. My schedule was from eight in the morning to three in the afternoon. We had some professional summer leagues, and I also went out for the Delaware Wings. It wasn't a great experience for me. We got very little pay and lots of responsibilities.

At that time, the Philadelphia Spartans were playing in the professional league. They had many local players, and I joined them although I was approaching the end of my playing career. They had Diego Burbano, Lenny Hoffman, Walt Tarnawski, Victor Hoffman, Dr. Lenny Bruce, and some other local players coached by George Montag. We played a lot of good games. We defeated the Boston team that had Bum Barbosa, a Brazilian high scorer. We beat them with a cross done by me to the head of Diego Burbano. This club also gave me the opportunity of being ejected for the first time in my entire professional career. We went to play a team in Falls River, Massachusetts. The game was being televised when on one play I faked out one of the opposing players in such a way that he took a fall. I didn't realize that he became very upset, and as I went to help him up, he suddenly punched me in the face. It didn't knock me down, but I just couldn't take that abuse. I went after that player and punched him back. Luckily, it was one of their best players who threw the punches so he also got ejected. We managed to win that game, and the ejections ended up helping us.

Our goalie, Walt Tarnawski, was complaining of a toothache, and he did not want to play. At the same time, Lenny Bilous had driven to the game and suffered an accident. I suggested that we talk to Walt; after all, you don't need to play soccer with your teeth. We convinced Walter to play regardless of his toothache. Lenny sat half of the game because all that was left of his car was left in his hands. Many things happened when teams travel, some things I can mention and some things I can't. We joked a lot inside the bus; sometimes the joker wasn't too funny.

George Montag was a good friend of mine. He was at that time a player coach. So during some of the games, he would get in there and play as well as the rest of the team. George did a lot for soccer in Philadelphia. He coached, played, and carried many teams to championships. I give him a lot of credit for helping the growth of soccer in the Philadelphia area. Presently, he is not doing too well, but I hope that he surpasses his health problems. In my opinion, George should get into the National Hall of Fame. He is always out watching games and expressing his opinions about different players that he coached. I thought he did a great job when he was coaching the Spartans. There are very few coaches I cared for while playing, but George Montag is a great coach and a great soccer representative for the city of Philadelphia.

While I was playing, I was also coaching high schools and colleges. I was teaching Spanish at Cardinal Dougherty High School, but the job there was difficult because they had a soccer coach who also worked at the school and was winning most of his games. I am referring to Jack Smith, the coach who gave Dougherty many championships. There I had very little chance even if I was a former national player, so I applied at Monsignor Bonner High School. They were interested, so I coached there from 1972 to 1976. We won Southern Division championships all of those years. We had a young and strong team; I spent a lot of extra time working with the team. The last season we had playoff games against our Northern Division championship opponents who were Archbishop Ryan, Cardinal Dougherty, and North Catholic. The last game we played North Catholic, we defeated them on our field 1 to 0. The players from North sat in our field facing the building and throwing rocks at it. It was a big upset in those days. St. Joseph's Prep was our toughest enemy. They were commanded by Jim Murray. Our games were hard, but we won most of the games even if riots were involved.

One weekend my wife and I were invited to a banquet at Bonner High School after winning the soccer Divisional Championship. It was a lot of fun, but there was one thing that got me upset. There was nothing said about soccer. My wife even noticed. It was all about American football. I decided on that day not to coach there because I felt that they did not give soccer the recognition it deserves. Of course, it was a decision that did not do me any good.

I then applied to Spring Garden College with the help of a friend Jose Palma, got interviewed, and got the job. At Spring Garden, there were nine scholarships available. I spent some of my time scouting, and because I was running a team in USL of Pa called Brasilia, I used some of the players during off-season. I got lucky getting some real good players from Cardinal Dougherty and Bonner. Somehow I managed to coach all three teams at one point. That doesn't leave much room for anything else. I took some players from Bonner that were turned down from other colleges and started building a team to compete for the championship of Division 19. From okaying on a muddy, disgraceful field, we went to a college field that was grassy and regular-sized.

For the size of Spring Garden College, we played some of the higher-ranking schools in the country on our schedule. We had Textile, who was among the top three in the country. We had Howard University, who was also highly ranked. We played them both and tied 3 to 3. The most important moment with Spring Garden was winning the Division 19 Championship. We defeated George Mason University at their own field 1 to 0. They filmed us and studied our team, but I had my players well-trained to get there. Many things happened during four seasons that lasted until 1980. Then I took a year off and went to Brazil.

While in Brazil, I went to the American School to teach English to a group of Japanese students, who were getting ready to come to the United Stated to go to college. It was a great experience dealing with the Japanese students. They were dedicated to their work, which made my job so much easier. There were no discipline problems, and they were using my book, *A New Approach to English*. They did very well. The Japanese were children of very important people.

They came to the American school driven in limousines. My car was the oldest car in the parking lot. I believe I did a good job with those kids. They were the best students I had in my life.

CHAPTER TWENTY

After playing professional soccer until 1975, I descended in my career to the amateur level. We were playing lower division ball because the players cared more about the game than the league that they played for. They were playing for their love of the sport. We had a Brazilian team in Philadelphia run by a Brazilian gentleman named Ubirajara Baldomero. He spent his money putting the team in the United Soccer League, which was run by Germans. They found so many grudges against any of the teams that weren't German. Every meeting, they were ready to give warnings for one reason or another.

We had three divisions. There was first, second, and third. Teams would start in the third division and move up if they won their division. Some made it in three years. We had fans that came to watch the games every Sunday. The games were listed in the local paper, and they showed interest in what was being done in the seventies. The local papers were interested in the development of the game. We had the German Major Clubs in the area with strong teams competing in the amateur and open cups. These German Clubs had their own fields. They should have dominated the league, but some of them came close to being lowered to the bottom divisions. There were some outstanding players that never made it to the professional teams. Most coaches had no interest in looking anywhere for any good player who was right here in the USA. I attended the league's meetings and knew enough German to know what they were doing.

During the presidency of Mr. Aldo D'Aversa, the treasury that held the money was suspected of missing large amounts of money. The board of directors decided to put their own money to have the league continue their schedule. After that problem, the league continued until the German clubs decided to go to the intercountry soccer league. It was the worst period for the United Soccer League to lose the Ukrainians, Phoenix Soccer Club, Erzgebirge, and the United German Hungarians.

Due to this event, I became a candidate to the presidency of the USL of Pennsylvania. I ran for president against Adam Mates who was German and also the president of Danubia Soccer Club, which was the only German club to stay with the league. When I became president, I was left with trying to keep the league alive and going at it the best way possible. I went around the city looking for new teams. We welcomed the foreign element back and had some Spanish, Africans, and Albanians, amongst others. We had twelve teams in the league, and we were doing fine. Soon enough, we got money to continue the league. The German clubs considered us defeated. They were surprised to find out that we still existed and were doing well. Those teams really abandoned the United Soccer League and fought us openly to close down, but I maneuvered around their negativity and kept the league intact moving forward. I did this for fifteen years. There were opportunities for the clubs to return, but they refused until some years ago. For whatever reasons, all of these clubs returned to the USL of Pennsylvania. I had made that promise, and now it came true. As soon as my promises were fulfilled, I wanted to get out of the league; and as a natural progression, other people were elected.

As an active president, I never presented a bill to the league. I have done my job with love, honor, and responsibility. I refuse to comment on other people involved. Once I felt that enough was enough, I stopped my participation with the league. I still came away from there with good friends such as Barry Strube and Werner Fricker Jr.

While I was president, I cultivated the indoor soccer for the winter. After I left, this idea was killed due to lack of interest by the board. As much as I love soccer, it is a different world to be inside a league like the USL of Pennsylvania. I kept my team in it for close to twenty years, changing its name from Brasilia to America to be able to welcome all nationalities to play; and believe me, I did have it. Later, I found a sponsor called the Kolping House, and the team's name became America Kolping. Under that name, we won one championship when my two sons, Alex Jr. and Ed, were played for me.

The United Soccer League of Pennsylvania had their own referee assigner; and during that time, they were doing fine. When the decision was made to hire an outside assigner to run the league's male or female games, they were very tough and deliberate on their purposes and actions. In my opinion, they were a hardship to the league and to the development of soccer. The USL of Pennsylvania is an affiliate to the USFA and FIFA. I failed to see that many people occupying offices were helping the growth of soccer in any way. I warned the league many times that if they did not change their attitude, someday it may die. I would need a new book to recall the sad episodes I had with bad referees. I know that the United States Soccer Federation could not control this herd of referees that were abundant in many playing sights.

My recollection of some of these episodes saddens my life because they totally degraded the sport of soccer. The EPSA had possession of thousands of dollars that came from their fines and from broken regulations. When the fines came, they were heavy-duty. I can't imagine an amateur league that fines the teams as if they were professionals. I feel that the USL of Pennsylvania is still alive today due to some of my personal efforts while the teams that are there now had abandoned them.

CHAPTER TWENTY-ONE

n 1996, I was in Jerry's Bar on Laurel and Lower Market Street in Northern Liberties in Philadelphia. The bar is between Spring Garden and Girard Avenue between Front and Second Street. Jerry Lebid was my assistant coach when I coached at Archbishop Carroll and Swarthmore College. We were talking about how people make it into the Hall of Fame for soccer. He suggested that I should be in it; after all, I had done as much if not more for the sport than people that were already in there. I thought that you have to be connected with the big shots around soccer. I remember being a good friend with Werner Friecker who was then the president of the United States Soccer Federation. I called Werner and asked him for an application to the Hall of Fame. I didn't have anything to lose because I felt that people forget quickly about the events in soccer. I was surprised to know that there were many team photos that included me in them around the federation. I was also surprised that anybody cared about the players from the sixties. We had some of our games televised, but I had never seen any of them. My life was always an investment in soccer. I had the grace of God helping me with life's other activities, but soccer is the game that kept me alive all of those years.

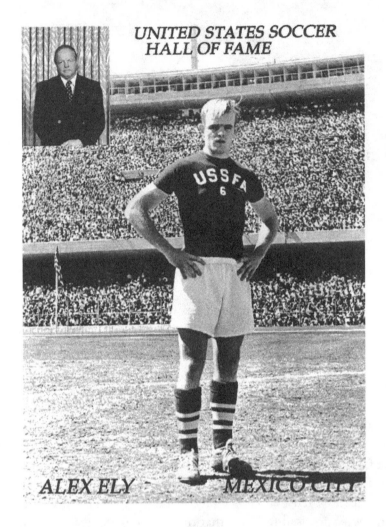

UNITED STATES SOCCER
HALL OF FAME

USSFA
6

ALEX ELY   MEXICO CITY

I remembered saying my prayers before every game. My honest wishes were to always play a good game and to respect my opponents. Sometimes during the games, one tends to forget about respect. I don't remember all of my actions during any given name. It was like pushing out everything inside my heart and putting forth my best effort. I do however remember clearly not having an attitude against teams, countries, or players. I respected the Cubans and Haitians as well as Brazilian and Argentinians. I never gave up during a game even when we got crushed when we played England in New York. If a player was good against me, I would try to mark him closer and try to prevent him from playing a good game against me.

Soccer involves reading what you are up against and trying to prevent it from happening. I remember during my amateur years when we played more organized teams and got crushed by high scores. What makes a person tick when the events are on? I never minded sitting on the bench because my heart was out there as if I was always in the game. Only God knows what goes on inside of each individual player. That is one of the reasons organized teams assemble prior to games to pray or to gain the confidence necessary to play a good game. I also played with great respect to the public that came to see us. Deep in my heart, I wanted them to go home happy with our performance.

There are certain players that attract bad luck, and they need to support to help overcome their bad luck. To be a good player, one needs to have his mind in the game. When we played internationally, my mind was devoted to the game from the moment the national anthems were played until the final whistle was blown by the referee. I also greatly admired the respected referees for it is one of the hardest jobs in the game. For these reasons, when I presented the USA, I was never fouled or even given warnings by the referees. My sliding tackles were always clean and on the ball.

After sending my application in 1996, it took a few months to find out if my qualifications were good enough to be inducted into the Hall of Fame. I was very surprised when they accepted me although I am a humble person and somehow thought I wasn't entitled to it. I started asking people that knew me, and they felt that I definitely deserved it, so I accepted, hoping to be a model for many young people.

We were invited to Harwick College in Oneonta, New York, for the induction ceremony and banquet. My name appeared in the newspapers again. I invited my family and some friends. It was a beautiful afternoon as I became a Hall of Famer forever. In my speech, I recall mentioning where I was born, about growing up, and my luck of getting selected to play the Pan American, Olympic, and World Cup eliminations, along with the success that we had at the time. I am referring to the sixties when I was selected to represent the United States.

Many people are curious to find out what it takes for a player to get into the Hall of Fame. There are a great number of ingredients needed to accomplish this. I shall name a few although I know the list will be incomplete. Being humble is definitely high on the list. A player should not brag about himself and be able to accept praises as well as criticism with an open mind. One example of this virtue is the great Pelé.

Always be honest with your friends and enemies alike. Do not start waves or talk against your own teammates or others no matter how bad they are. This is the job of the coaching and management. I've seen many good players sink through that hole. Because they play good, they immediately want to run the team. Making coaching suggestions and thus forcing coaches out of clubs, and eventually these players get burned out.

Don't be a brownnoser; people don't respect that. Don't go hanging around the coaches and embarrass them if they ever feel like sitting with you or one of your friends. Don't take other people's pains or anger. This is very common in soccer. There are players that feel that their friends should play rather than respecting the coaches' decision.

Don't be jealous of others even if they get all the attention from the newspapers, magazines, or television. Many players get irate when the attention is directed toward other players. Don't worry about that, follow this advice, and your day will come.

Play for the team; pass the ball to whoever is open and do not pass it to him just because he is your friend. I've seen many players do that and sometimes lose the ball instead of passing it to the player who was open. That is not the way to go. By looking at a player during a game, you can determine what kind of man he is.

I also advise players to be courageous and to take chances with shots on goal. In my mind, if you don't shoot, you can't score. Always believe that you can get to the ball before your opponent. These game details help to build a personality which can't be touched by anybody during a game. Unfortunately, many players are not educated and came from poor neighborhoods around the world.

When I was in Santos FC in 1965, I was teaching interested players English. They were interested, but some of them had a hard time with their own language. I feel that the teams should provide some education and etiquette to their players. Today, we see players making millions who don't care about their education. Pelé was always trying to improve his education. I consider myself lucky to have had the opportunity to graduate from college and earn a master's degree to advance in my career.

CHAPTER TWENTY-TWO

Many young Americans love soccer, and the game is definitely number one in their lives. As soon as they are able to realize that there is more of a future in baseball, basketball, or American football, their attitudes begin to change toward the game that they left behind. Among the problems is that very few Americans are interested in a future with soccer because it is next to impossible to make the big-time soccer. Most of our promising players are playing in Europe due to lack of interest here mostly for the experience, which they will achieve there.

When I was playing in Brazil, I played a few games for a team called Black Power. There were only black players on that team, but they made an exception for me. After all, my father was one of the founders of the Vila Brasilio Machado. Many times I was invited to their club. They had dances on the weekends. I never went to those dances, but I did attend one of their evening demonstrations in the neighborhood. They treated me greatly. I was special for many of them because I grew up there, and I had achieved something good with soccer. I felt honored walking from tent to tent being greeted as someone of importance. I felt good with them and wanted to do something to help them. I tried to bring one of their players to America, but it did not work out. I feel that a friend is a friend, and I never made any distinction in my life.

In the USA, my own soccer team called America Kolping was always populated with people of many different backgrounds. I have had Brazilians, Latins, Africans, Haitians, Jamaicans, Irish, and this provoked the league. They treated us with considerable prejudice for the continuous years that we participated. Today some of the German clubs have black players, I believe, thanks to our efforts.

Many good things have resulted through friendships in the years I devoted to the USL of Pennsylvania. Because of living through all these problems, I became stronger in my beliefs. America was the name I chose for my team because I believe that anybody from anywhere in the world can be made welcome using soccer as their sport.

I know many people who love soccer and are continuously supporting it by donating time and money to different teams. One of these gentlemen is a fan of the Portuguese Benfica FC and a great supporter of all soccer activities. His name is Filinto Marques. He respects me for being in the National Hall of Fame and for my dedication to soccer. I am sure that my instincts do not coincide with many other people involved in the game. Every team that I played for had some kind of problem. A lot of these problems were due to lack of education. When I started teaching English to the professionals of Santos FC in Brazil, many newspapers captured the idea of having some sort of schooling to help athletes grow mentally and physically. While coaching in college, I wandered around many campuses in the United States. I've met many good players who were pursuing an education and were very good students sometimes with honors. It surprised me to find out that soccer players had the better grades in a lot of these colleges. Because they know that you can't make a good living out of soccer.

Today, Americans face this exodus of players to other countries where the game is more popular. Our coaches have the guts of selecting the outsiders over the boys who stay here, hoping for a chance when there is none or very few. I feel that soccer is a game that you don't learn in schools. Each individual player develops his talent watching and learning his own way from the better players. A good coach can take these players and improve them in many ways with training and proper positioning on the field. A coach is needed to improve, guide, and set the team's structure in all field activities. Coaching is difficult because of the pressure from the clubs and management for good results. I also believe that a good coach has to be able to make decisions on and off the field concerning a player's well-being. Sometimes these decisions can be painful. Sometimes good coaches make decisions that can hurt the team more than it helps. Regardless, he or she has to live with these decisions.

The USFA should bring the right kind of coaches with the right veteran players and give them jobs with the youth teams. They could teach them their skills and be more active with their growth into the world of soccer. What we have to do in the United States is to promote the game as they do in any soccer country in the world and let the game be a joy to all the people who love it. I also believe that players should be paid salaries that are sensible; there should be a limit to their heights in soccer and in all other sports. Today we have players earning more than the presidents of many countries. They should have a limit to what a player can earn based on the economic factor. I am not only referring to soccer but to all sports. With salary that is offered, it becomes more interesting to become a professional player than to become a president. All pro players should get very good pay but not exceeding an agreed amount that would leave enough money for the people to attend the games affordably. As the entrance price goes up and the economy goes down, fewer people will be able to attend many of the professional games. It has become difficult for me, as I imagine it has become for others. The owners want their money, and the only way to raise it is by charging the public.

CHAPTER TWENTY-THREE

The Public

What does the public want to see in a soccer game? First, I'd like to see my favorite team winning. Second, I'm paying to see a good competition, and I would still be happy whether my team wins or loses.

From my experience and the years I played for the US, the public that supported us was minimal. Recently, I went to see the United States play Honduras for a World Cup qualifying match in Philadelphia. I felt as if I were in Honduras. There were twenty-five thousand people in the stadium, and all I saw was a sea of Honduran faces dominating the crowd. We are not selling our product. The Hondurans came out of the woodwork to see their country trying to reach the World Cup. The United States won the game, and there were hardly any celebrations, or at least I didn't see any.

During the time that I played for the Ukrainians, we had most of the community supporting the team. They carried flags, signs, or any identifying item that showed that they were rooting for us. That wasn't seen in any other team that competed against us. Not only did they come out to the stadium to see us play, but it felt as if they genuinely cared about us. That was displayed by their respectful attitude toward us by helping us get jobs and feel more comfortable in the US. If there were any players who were injured, they found a way to fund our medical care and any other aspects of life that needed to be dealt with. I suffered several bad injuries but somehow always made it back on the team. There were some players who didn't have any such luck and never made it back. The team continues to play with or without you.

I have learned a valuable lesson: do not play if you are injured. The results can be dangerous for you and could hurt your game forever.

The public knows you from the field; some like you, and some don't. I was very fortunate to be liked by the fans. They learn to trust you as a player in the games that they watch. My own evaluations come from talking and listening. Some will see you as the savior of the team or as the guy you can always rely on to make the play. There are some people who are constant critics of players and games. I give them credit.

I learned a lot about the fans after the injuries I sustained. Once you are not playing, the public generally feels sorry for you. They will constantly ask how you are feeling. No matter what your answer is, they do not believe you. Each time that I returned to the lineup, I was a different man. I became more solid and indifferent to the public's view. I wasn't as friendly anymore. I was thinking of myself and how it felt to be able to overcome the injury and make the public believe in me again. I was fortunate for being able to perform well enough to draw their attention to me again.

In 1959, during the Pan American Games in Chicago, the public was relatively small; but regardless of that, we did really well, earning the third place out of seven countries. We lost two games, and one was against Argentina. The other was against Costa Rica. The public that followed us was very satisfied with our playing ability, plus we were representing the US, so many of us fought harder to win those games. The fans who followed us were very happy indeed.

For the first time, that team defeated Brazil soundly by a 5-3 win. That fact made no history in the USA, but in Brazil, the media explored that miracle to no end. When I played in Canada for Toronto Roma, the public there did not accept defeat. They wanted you to win all the time. If you lost a game, it wasn't a good idea to go to the club and try to get paid. The fans were furious, parading up and down the streets in Toronto. When Toronto Roma played in Toronto Italia in 1960, the mounted police surrounded the field, most of them riding horses. Wherever there was a display of animosity, the police went and arrested the angry fans. They wound up missing the game, and that was enough punishment for a fanatic.

In 1960, we played the first round of the World Cup qualification match in Los Angeles against Mexico. We were at home. Out of thirty-five thousand attendants, twenty-five were Mexican. It did not feel as though we had a home field advantage. In Mexico, the stadium was filled completely; there were people hanging on the flagpole. The US management sent us to play at noon, and that was when the heat and humidity were at their peak. We could hardly breathe due to the altitude of Mexico City. Such a game should never take place at that scheduled hour. Our players tried very hard, but it was impossible to overcome those conditions even though we had oxygen on the sidelines for people to catch their breath every so often. This event was scheduled due to agreements between the US Federation and the Mexican Federation who knew the whole time what we would be up against. Their excuse was that the game would interfere with the bullfights, which were to be held at three o'clock. Most of the players felt cheated, but as soon as the game was over, the people responsible were nowhere to be found.

I was short of money, but I had a return ticket and left for New York as soon as a flight became available. I went to the US Federation there and borrowed money for my return trip to Philadelphia. I was billed for it a few weeks later.

My name was published in the Mexican newspapers, and I was receiving offers to play there. Since I was in college, I thought it was a better idea to stay there at that stage in my life. The games for the 1966 World Cup elimination were better. We had some time to prepare for them in Bermuda. We ended up in a 2-2 tie here. After seeing the public in Mexico and the newspapers reporting on all of the US players, we returned to the US, and there was nobody waiting at the airport to greet us. That made me recall a time when I was playing for the Ukrainians and returned from a game we played for the Lewis Cup. The Ukrainians were waiting for us at three o'clock in the morning and gave us a great reception. It was an all-night celebration.

Upon returning to the US in 1965, there was nothing significant happening in the US. That was when the USSF selected me as the best player in the USA and honored me with a banquet. These are some moments in life that you never forget. I encompass all of these events, as a young kid practicing balls by breaking three-inch bricks in my forehead to become a good head ball-hitter in my playing days. My wishes of best luck to all people interested in soccer.

Mia Hamm and Alex Ely

CPSIA information can be obtained
at www.ICGtesting.com
Printed in the USA
LVHW110737241220
674973LV00005B/811